Exploring
Nonfiction Literacies

Exploring Nonfiction Literacies

Innovative Practices in Classrooms

Edited by
Vivian Yenika-Agbaw,
Ruth McKoy Lowery,
Laura Anne Hudock,
and Paul H. Ricks

ROWMAN & LITTLEFIELD
Lanham • Boulder • New York • London

Published by Rowman & Littlefield
A wholly owned subsidiary of The Rowman & Littlefield Publishing Group, Inc.
4501 Forbes Boulevard, Suite 200, Lanham, Maryland 20706
www.rowman.com

Unit A, Whitacre Mews, 26-34 Stannary Street, London SE11 4AB

British Library Cataloguing in Publication Information Available

Library of Congress Cataloging-in-Publication Data

Library of Congress Cataloging-in-Publication Data Available

ISBN 978-1-4758-4341-5 (cloth)
ISBN 978-1-4758-4342-2 (pbk.)
ISBN 978-1-4758-4343-9 (electronic)

Contents

Figures

Tables

Acknowledgments

This professional contribution would not have been possible without the support from our families, friends, colleagues, administrators, and the interlibrary loan staff at the Pennsylvania State University, who made sure we had access to the relevant professional resources in a timely manner. In addition, a special thank-you goes to Tom Koerner, whose faith in the project, and constant encouragement, kept us focused; and to the Rowman & Littlefield production and editorial teams, especially Carlie Wall and Emily Tuttle, for their guidance throughout the project.

A book is nothing without the dedication of its authors; thus, we thank all the contributors who worked diligently on their chapters and responded in a timely manner to editorial reminders to bring this project to fruition. Additionally, we wish to thank Barbara Kiefer and Leigh Brodsky-Schubert for agreeing to write blurbs for this book at short notice.

Introduction

Critical Thinkers and Innovative Practices

Vivian Yenika-Agbaw and Ruth McKoy Lowery

> When I asked the teachers I work with why nonfiction literature was not an integral part of their daily read-alouds, their answers were unilateral. Although more than 98% acknowledged that they didn't do enough read-alouds with nonfiction, 75% of these teachers didn't have or know how to locate appropriate nonfiction materials to read to their children. (Stead, 2014, p. 489)

Young learners live each day inquisitively exploring the world around them through questioning. They often ask questions about how their world functions, asking "why" questions that sometimes frustrate the adults in their lives. Why is the ball round? Why is the sky blue? Why did my dog die? Why do I have to go to sleep? Why does my tummy hurt? The list becomes longer and more complicated as they get older and experience new things around them. For some of these children, a simple answer, even if not fully understood, is enough to stymie their curiosity for a while.

For others, they keep probing, sincerely seeking to understand how the greater world outside themselves exist. Our participation in the global world, however, demands that young children be engaged in meaningful ways that prepare them to be contributing members of our diverse society. The tenets of this book advocate for critical and innovative practices that engage readers with nonfiction children's literature and/or texts. As such, a healthy dose of skepticism is not always a "bad" thing!

As classroom teachers seek to expand their students' knowledge, capitalizing on their zest for learning and finding captivating materials to motivate them with, children's books, particularly nonfiction literature, offer an array of topics for this exploration. The integration of nonfiction texts in schools' curricula has gained marked attention as more and more teachers are expected to expose their students to this genre. Overwhelmingly, however, Stead (2014) posits that many of these teachers often complain that they do not know how to access these materials. Stead determines that reading nonfiction books aloud to children can help stimulate their interests. Not only should nonfiction literature be read for content learning, but it should also be utilized for students' reading enjoyment, and for other purposes determined by students.

Nonfiction, when utilized in meaningful ways, can be educational, enjoyable, and serve as a powerful tool that transforms students' learning in and out of the classroom. Through a vast array of nonfiction materials, this goal can be achieved. A major goal of this book is to discuss how learners might be guided to interact with texts in a creative but critically engaged and sustainable manner.

Contributors recognize nonfiction text as a staple of the literacy curriculum and advocate that educators adopt a critical mindset and a risk-taking approach toward their daily practices. Thus, the book offers what we consider innovative ideas on how nonfiction texts can be used to nurture literacy acquisition, growth, and fluency in and out of the classroom.

STEPPING INTO NONFICTION

The history of nonfiction children's literature dates to 1657 with the publication of *Orbis Pictus* by Johann Amos Comenius. This book was created as a picture dictionary illustrated with woodcuts and was used as a textbook throughout Europe until the late eighteenth century. Hence, it served a dual purpose, being both nonfiction and a picture book. For many young children, this was their sole means of educational development. They were admonished to be good citizens, and presenting nonfiction materials to them was one way in which these values were instilled.

Over time, as children's literature became a staple in learning, the focus shifted to presenting "fun" reading materials, preferably fairy tales and other fictitious stories. However, in the last three decades, nonfiction literature has been championed and encouraged as a staple in schools' curricula, becoming a more popular and important genre in children's literature. The advent of the Orbis Pictus Award for nonfiction, created by the National Council of Teachers of English in 1989, has provided a concrete resource for finding the latest and best in nonfiction children's literature. According to Jensen (2001), the award sought to honor books that met criteria related to accuracy, organization, design, and style.

In recent years, the National Council of Teachers of English has incorporated various ways to bring the Orbis Pictus Award winners to a wider education audience in hopes that young readers have the opportunity to explore the greater world through these materials. However, we should also err on the side of caution by nurturing readers in deliberate ways so they not only cultivate an inquiring mindset but one that is critical as well.

BEING CRITICAL ABOUT NONFICTION

Shannon (2007) advocates three steps in being critical about the texts we read. They involve reading beyond the surface meaning to examine the social meanings of texts, asking evocative and profound questions to determine why things are the way they are, and acting on the new knowledge gained from interrogating the text (p. 1). As young readers explore the world around them through nonfiction literature, they can learn to read with a critical lens that helps them to grasp the materials they learn and to expand the meanings they construct from their multiple encounters with texts. They are also able to find the answers to the many questions they ask; if not, they can continue to research.

Readers learn to be civic citizens engaged in examining their world through the lens of accuracy, organization, design, and style advocated by the Orbis Pictus. They also learn to forge connections across disciplines. Teachers can engage them in a plethora of activities to critically determine the text's viability.

Some things to consider as teachers select nonfiction materials include the author's qualification to write about the topic, the accuracy of the information presented, the sources of the information, and the presentation of the information. These factors are important in presenting factual information to young readers. The material should be vetted and clearly researched to minimize misinformation.

BEING INNOVATIVE WITH NONFICTION TEXTS

Educators can deepen students' learning about their world through practices that go beyond the ordinary ways of doing school and/or doing life. In this book, we refer to such practices as innovative, "featuring new methods; advanced or original" (Oxford Dictionary https://en.oxforddictionaries.com /definition/innovative). These are practices that challenge learners to see the world from a new perspective and to notice the continuity in learning that occurs in the classroom and that occurs in other spaces initiated by them and/ or supported by an adult.

Such practices also make familiar literacy activities new in order to push our thinking. They help us educators to rethink the classroom as a space of possibilities, even with all the constraints that are usually associated with such formal spaces. Moreover, they push us to take advantage of learners' social worlds outside the classroom and what they have to offer to the curious learner, considering these spaces as playgrounds for complex literacy events. In this way, activities in these varied settings might inadvertently expand our understanding of what might be considered other kinds of nonfiction texts.

Learners' transactions with traditional nonfiction children's literature are enhanced by the connections they are able to make to other kinds of nonfiction texts within their surrounding communities. And this is only possible when educators think beyond, challenge learners to see beyond, to strive beyond, and to create new meanings from their multiple interactions and transactions with these texts. Contributors to this book share ideas on how to rethink discussion that is often a staple in literature-based literacy curriculum; offer exciting ideas on how to extend experiences with nonfiction literature; but also remind readers of certain foundational practices that undergird the innovative practices we espouse.

OVERVIEW OF THE BOOK

There are seven chapters in this book, excluding this introduction and the conclusion, that put nonfiction literature and literacies into perspective. Chapter 1 provides a brief history of nonfiction/biographies, discussing topics that are under exploration and the wealth of resources that exist and challenge educators to rethink their practices in order to stimulate young learners' inquiring minds.

Chapter 2 discusses how picture book biographies can provide a template for diverse learners to construct autobiographies reflective of their personal interests and cultural backgrounds. Furthermore, it recommends creating spaces within the curriculum around these mentor texts that afford learners ample opportunities to embark on design-thinking projects that place them in the driver's seat.

Chapters 3, 4, and 5 center specific groups of learners and specific populations of interest in books: the gifted and/or English language learners (ELLs;

also referred to by some educators as multilingual learners). In chapter 3, the authors describe their experiences working with gifted learners to understand the complexities of nonfiction texts and how these engagements transform their students' learning of content and enhance their skills as meaning makers and/or constructors of meanings. It also discusses how learners apply skill sets to other settings.

Chapter 4, on the other hand, discusses the different kinds of disabilities that are being explored in picture books, explaining why certain disabilities seem to dominate and why others are not mentioned. The authors share their experience working with learners on this topic and the possibilities that thoughtful activities that invite learners to empathize might offer.

Chapter 5 presents ideas on how educators might use nonfiction for teaching academic content and complex English language concepts to ELLs. It also explains why it is necessary to create a harmonious atmosphere that accommodates the needs of both ELLs and mainstream learners through a careful selection of nonfiction texts.

Chapter 6 discusses the pedagogical strengths of multimodal text sets in a literacy curriculum and offers ideas on how educators might integrate text sets across curriculum to teach content and reinforce skill sets. Chapter 7 shares ideas for creating aesthetically pleasing classroom libraries with high-quality nonfiction texts to foster critical thinking.

Together, the chapters in this book form a useful compilation of educational materials for teachers, students, and other stakeholders. As we advocate for the integration of nonfiction texts in schools' curricula, we attempt to offer what we believe to be worthwhile ideas from diverse perspectives that readers might find useful as they design experiences and consider strategies for doing this work. The incorporation of nonfiction texts across content areas and in multiple formats, and for enjoyment, helps students to learn about the greater world outside their lived experiences.

This book is important in that it highlights how this integration can be made accessible across age and grade levels. It is our hope that we have provided some of the basic tools for teachers to engage their students with nonfiction texts in innovative ways. The philosophical stance that continues to inform our practice as educators is one of seeing ALL learners as capable! To enable their potential, we must go the extra mile to make literature/literacy events relevant, exciting, and purposeful, and to encourage them to develop an inquiring mind set. As we completed this book the NCTE Orbis Pictus committee had just announced the 2018 award-winning title and honor books. See textbox I.1 for the list of books.

TEXTBOX I.1

"NCTE ORBIS PICTUS OUTSTANDING NONFICTION FOR CHILDREN"

Chin, Jason (2017). *Grand Canyon*. New York: Roaring Book Press. (2018 Winner)

Honor Books:

- *Chef Roy Choi and the Street Food Remix* by Jacqueline Briggs Martin and June Jo Lee, illustrated by Man One (Readers to Eaters)
- *Dazzle Ships: World War I and the Art of Confusion* by Chris Barton, illustrated by Victo Ngai (Millbrook Press)
- *Her Right Foot* by Dave Eggers, illustrated by Shawn Harris (Chronicle Books LLC)
- *The Quilts of Gee's Bend* by Susan Goldman Rubin (ABRAMS)
- *The World is Not a Rectangle: A Portrait of Architect Zaha Hadid* by Jeanette Winter (Beach Lane Books)

Recommended Books:

- *Danza! Amalia Hernández and El Ballet Folklórico de México* by Duncan Tonatiuh (Dreamscape Media)
- *Fault Lines in the Constitution* by Cynthia Levinson & Sanford Levinson (Peachtree Publishers, Ltd.)
- *If Sharks Disappeared* by Lily Williams (Roaring Brook Press)
- *Isaac the Alchemist: Secrets of Isaac Newton, Reveal'd* by Mary Losure (Candlewick Press)
- *Life on Surtsey: Iceland's Upstart Island* by Loree Griffin Burns (Houghton Mifflin Harcourt)
- *Maya Lin: Thinking With Her Hands* by Susan Goldman Rubin (Chronicle Books LLC)
- *The Music of Life: Bartolomeo Cristofori & the Invention of the Piano* by Elizabeth Rusch, illustrated by Marjorie Priceman (Atheneum Books for Young Readers)
- *The Whydah: A Pirate Ship Feared, Wrecked, and Found* by Martin W. Sandler (Candlewick Press)"

Source: Retrieved from the website December 2, 2017: http://www2.ncte.org/awards/orbis-pictus -award-nonfiction-for-children/

REFERENCES

Jensen, J. M. (2001). "The quality of prose in Orbis Pictus award books." In M. Zarnowski, R. Kerper, and J. M. Jensen. *The best in children's nonfiction: Reading, writing, & teaching Orbis Pictus Award books*, 3–12. Urbana, IL: National Council of Teachers of English.

Shannon, P. (2007). "Critical literacy and everyday life." *New England Reading Association* 43(2), 1–5.

Stead, T. (2014). "Nurturing the inquiring mind through the nonfiction read-aloud." *The Reading Teacher* 67(7), 488–95.

Chapter One

Exploring the Universe of Facts

Outstanding Nonfiction and Biographies for Children

Deborah Thompson

With the advent of "post-truths," "alternative facts," and "fake news," it is significant that young readers are naturally attracted to the natural world and books that explain that world. Their curiosity leads them to select books that explain and inform—nonfiction, the genre of real facts. Dinosaurs, beetles, cats, airplanes, butterflies, the solar system, and real people excite young readers and motivate them to seek out books on such topics online, in libraries, and in bookstores. That children gravitate toward the universe of real facts has been noted by children's literature scholars.

Nonfiction has gained in popularity over the past one hundred years, with some of the biggest growth coming in the 1970s and 1980s (Giblin, 2000). Also, changes in curricular approaches to teaching and the implementation of the Common Core English Language Arts Standards have fueled the current nonfiction boom (Rosen, 2013).

In a definitive work, Giblin (2000) traces the nonfiction genre back to the turn of the twentieth century. He notes that pioneering educators and children's librarians sought to make nonfiction available for young readers because as one forward-looking expert noted, "there is poetry in jet planes and space ships and atoms" (p. 414).

Authors addressing children's insatiable need to know about things and people have produced disparate works, from the White Rose movement during World War II (Freedman, 2016) to the three-volume graphic nonfiction series *March: Book One* (Lewis and Aydin, 2013); *March: Book Two* (Lewis and Aydin, 2015); and *March: Book Three* (Lewis and Aydin, 2016).

The simplicity of a biography for young readers (most biographies are considered nonfiction) often belies the difficulties in writing a lively and readable life account. What to include? What to exclude? Don Brown (2007), author of many notable picture book biographies, focuses on important periods in a subject's life. Instead of giving fact after boring fact about a subject, Brown allows the seminal periods of a subject's life to guide his writing.

Russell Freedman (1994), recognized as one of the finest biographers of subjects for young readers, does meticulous research to write the "story" of the subject's life. He does not use the word *story* to mean he has made things up, but that he writes to "ignite the reader's imagination, evoking pictures and scenes in the reader's mind" (p. 139).

Biographers of children's works must be consummate researchers. They not only must present a well-rounded portrait of the subject, but also be students of the times and environment in which their subjects lived. The hallmark of an exemplary biography is a lively narrative supported by documented sources—especially primary sources. The presence of archival sources, bibliographies, endnotes, reading lists, and other documentation shows an author's respect for the reader and an invitation for "individual inquiry and critical thinking" (Carter 2003, p. 169).

Children's nonfiction, which for the purposes of this chapter will include biographies, provides young readers a world of opportunities to engage in critical thinking and explore the world around them. Exemplary nonfiction invites readers to immerse themselves in the universe of facts and gain a background of a myriad of topics—which in outstanding works must include thorough and accurate research, documented sources, and quotes with accurate attributions.

TRENDS IN NONFICTION—FORMAT

Children's literature is always evolving—from hybrid formats to graphic novels. Two formats that have been successfully introduced to the field are hybrids of poetry/nonfiction and poetry/biography and graphic nonfiction. Poetry/nonfiction hybrids can be lyrical and informative forms such as Joyce Sidman's *Before Morning* (2016). Poetry/nonfiction formats can also inform readers about significant world events and eras. Ashley Bryan (2016) uses original slave auction and plantation estate documents to re-create the lives of eleven enslaved Africans and the inhumanity of being priced, bought, and sold as personal property in *Freedom Over Me: Eleven Slaves, Their Lives and Dreams Brought to Life* .

Despite Jim Crow laws and rampant bigotry in the country and the military, African American soldiers fought with courage and valor on the battlefields of World War I. J. Patrick Lewis (2014) highlights the soldiers' experiences in *Harlem Hellfighters*, a book of nonfiction as poetry as opposed to nonfiction with poetry. Kadir Nelson's *Nelson Mandela* (2013) and Ntozake Shange's *Coretta Scott* (2009) are biographies in poetry form.

Charles R. Smith Jr.'s *28 Days: Moments in Black History That Changed the World* (2015) highlights twenty-eight significant black history events that forever changed American and world history—for example, November 4, 2008, when Barack Obama was elected the United States' first African American president. Wynton Marsalis's (2005) award-winning *Jazz ABZ: An A to Z Collection of Jazz Portraits* is a triple hybrid of poetry, alphabet book, and biography.

The poetry/biography hybrid is a perfect vehicle for life stories for older readers. Marilyn Nelson (2005) has perfected the poetry/biography hybrid in such award-winning titles as *A Wreath for Emmett Till*, in which she uses a heroic crown of sonnets—where the last line of one poem becomes the first line of the next poem—to tell the story of the lynching of Emmett Till. In *Carver, A Life in Poems*, Nelson (2001) uses poetry to tell the life story of George Washington Carver—ex-slave and outstanding agricultural scientist whose many inventions made life easier for everyone and farming more profitable for blacks and whites in the South. *The Freedom Business* (2008) is a narrative of the life of Ventura, an enslaved African, and *Sweethearts of Rhythm* (2009) tells in biographical poetry the story of what was at that time considered the greatest all-female band in the world.

Like Nelson, Margarita Engle uses the poetry/biography hybrid to perfection to give readers a view of the history of Cuba, unsullied by today's political machinations—see, for example, *The Poet Slave of Cuba* (2006). Carole Boston Weatherford uses poetry to tell the life stories of famed civil rights leaders Fannie Lou Hamer (2015) and Matthew Henson (2008), the African American explorer who discovered the North Pole (or who co-discovered the North Pole, depending on which version of history one reads). Patricia Hruby Powell (2014) won several awards, including a Sibert Honor Medal for the poetic life story of Josephine Baker, *Josephine: The Dazzling Life of Josephine Baker*.

Sanderson (2004) calls graphic nonfiction a "unique medium for presenting history and biography" (p. 14). British author/illustrator Marcia Williams is noted for adapting classic topics in a comic strip format. However, where Williams frames her classic cartoons in a variety of lively color palettes, today's graphic nonfiction selections are darker in tone in subject matter and color palettes. Don Brown's 2016 Orbis Pictus winner *Drowned City: Hurricane Katrina and New Orleans* (2015) is a dark and stark reporting of how an entire city was almost destroyed by a superstorm, broken levies, and disaster relief mismanagement from Mayor Nagin to President George W. Bush and his FEMA Director Michael Brown. Nothing about the disaster is sugarcoated.

Brown's pages are replete with dead bodies floating in debris-filled flood waters, people looting, people stranded on roofs, and people at the convention center and the Super Dome. For a disaster of this scope, graphic nonfiction is the perfect vehicle for portraying the wide-scale failure of the social safety net on multiple levels. Don Brown (2013) applies the graphic format to another widespread climate-related disaster—*The Great American Dustbowl*.

Congressman and civil rights icon John Lewis co-authored with Andrew Aydin a graphic trilogy of the civil rights movement. *March: Book One* (2013) covers Lewis's early years and the Nashville Student movement of which Lewis was a member. *March: Book Two* (2015) covers Lewis's rise in civil rights leadership and the historic 1963 March on Washington.

March: Book Three (2016) includes the bombing of the 16th Street Baptist Church; Freedom Summer, including the murders of three civil rights workers—Chaney, Goodman, and Schwerner; and the 1964 Democratic Convention. *March: Book Three* won several top literary prizes, including the National Book Award for Young People's Literature, the Coretta Scott King Author Award, and the Sibert Award.

TRENDING—LIFE STORIES OF INTREPID WOMEN

Everyone has a life story that evolves with each lived experience. Autobiography, biography, memoirs, and other personal narratives—for example, journals, diaries, or letters—provide entrée into some of these life stories, from the mundane to the highly individual. Duthie (1998) believes that biographies and autobiographies allow child readers "to gaze at the world through the eyes and experiences of others" (p. 220). Teachers, scientists, singers, explorers, cowboys, athletes, and many other ordinary citizens from a myriad of ethnic, racial, and cultural backgrounds have influenced world events and shaped history as it now stands.

Authenticity and accuracy are essential to writing good biographies for any reader, but especially for children. Moore (1985) warns authors that in their attempts to simplify and/or condense the material about well-known or not-so-well-known subjects, they must be careful not to give incomplete or inaccurate information. This entails writers consulting varied sources to create the most accurate picture of the subject.

The picture book biography is a good introduction to life stories for young readers. These biographies often focus on the childhood of famous people. As with any picture book, illustrations support the text to enhance the subject's life. Bader (2013) notes that at their best, picture book biographies can do what no other format can do. They have pictures that rivet the reader's attention, convey emotion, and imprint a moment. The text is beyond everyday words (p. 18).

Picture book biographies have brought to readers' attention the life stories of many intrepid women, some of whom are well known, such as Lena Horne (Weatherford, 2017), and others not so well known, such as the first woman to receive a medical degree in the United States, Elizabeth Blackwell (Stone, 2013), and pioneering Chinese American pilot, Maggie Gee (Moss, 2009). With the current emphasis on STEM subjects, there have been several picture book biographies published, on subjects such as Shark Lady Eugenia Clark, (Lang, 2016); the world's first computer programmer; Lord Byron's daughter, Ada Byron Lovelace (Robinson, 2016); and Marie Tharp, who mapped the ocean floor (Burleigh, 2016).

TEXTBOX 1.1

SELECTED PICTURE BOOK
BIOGRAPHIES OF INTREPID WOMEN

Look up! Henrietta Leavitt, pioneering woman astronomer (Burleigh, 2013)

Solving the puzzle under the sea: Marie Tharp maps the ocean floor (Burleigh, 2016)

Florence Nightingale (Demi, 2014)

Dare the wind: The record-breaking voyage of Eleanor Prentiss and the Flying Cloud (Fern, 2014)

Annie Jump Cannon, astronomer (Gerber, 2011)

The tree lady: The true story of how one tree-loving woman changed a city forever (Hopkins, 2013)

Swimming with the sharks: The daring discoveries of Eugenia Clark (Lang, 2016)

Caroline's comet: A true story (McCully, 2017)

Sky high: The true story of Maggie Gee (Moss, 2009)

Life in the ocean: The story of oceanographer Sylvia Earle (Nivola, 2012)

Wangari Maathai: The woman who planted millions of trees (Prévot, 2015)

Ada's ideas: The story of Ada Lovelace, the world's first computer programmer (Robinson, 2016)

Jars of hope: How one woman helped save 2,500 children during the Holocaust (Roy, 2015)

Who said women can't be doctors? (Stone, 2013)

The house that Jane built: A story about Jane Addams (Stone, 2015)

Dolores Huerta: A hero to migrant workers (Warren, 2012)

The legendary Miss Lena Horne (Weatherford, 2017)

Voice of freedom: Fannie Lou Hamer, spirit of the Civil Rights Movement (Weatherford, 2015)

Collective biographies are abbreviated thematic collections of life stories. These biographies focus on select aspects of the subjects' achievements. Collective biographies focus on every manner of individuals, from royal African princesses (Hansen, 2004) to pirates of the Caribbean and other bodies of water (Krull, 2010). Women have been intrepid from the earliest period of human existence, beginning with Lucy—the three-million-year-old female hominid (fossil) found in Ethiopia (Thimmesh, 2009). Women have served on the battlefront as correspondents during World War II (Colman, 2002; Gourley, 2007) and during that same war as field nurses and prisoners of war (Farrell, 2014). They bravely serve in the United States Senate and House of Representatives (Cooper, 2014). They are rabble-rousers (Harness, 2004) and scientists of renown (Lawlor, 2017).

Complete biographies often appeal to older children who want to discover more about a subject's entire life rather than abbreviated information found in picture book, partial, or collective biographies. Complete biographies also provide the chronological and historical context in which the subjects' accomplishments occurred.

Well-known biographies of intrepid women include *The Girl from the Tarpaper School: Barbara Rose Johns and the Advent of the Civil Rights Movement* (Kanefield, 2014), *Ida M. Tarbell: The Woman Who Challenged Big Business—and Won!* (McCully, 2014), and *Jeannette Rankin: Political Pioneer* (Woelfle, 2007). Jeannette Rankin, the first woman elected to the United States Congress, is most famously known for casting the only vote against the United States entering World War II (she was one of fifty who voted against the country's entering World War I)—intrepid indeed.

CURRENT NONFICTION AS A PLATFORM FOR SOCIAL JUSTICE

Social justice has as many definitions as there are people defining the term. It is a patchwork concept of equity and opportunities for all. Some definitions include the distribution of wealth, while others simply state that it means equal opportunities for all, especially for those in greatest need.

Given the generous and broad range of definitions there are for social justice, it is easy to conclude that the concept of social justice would necessarily encompass myriad issues and concerns, such as access to healthy food, water, and health care; freedom from war and strife; suffrage and ballot box access; climate change and care for the environment; marriage equality, civil rights, and immigration. Newly published nonfiction and biographies address many of these issues and more; therefore, in this section, nonfiction/biographies on the environment, particularly climate change, civil disobedience, and immigration will be highlighted.

Protecting Our Little Blue Marble

In December 1968, the astronauts of Apollo 8 became the first men to orbit the moon. During that mission on Christmas Eve, the astronauts captured the first picture of Earth as it appeared from deep space, rising above the horizon of the moon. Labeled the most important photograph in the twentieth century (Kluger, 2013), the snapshot, entitled *Earthrise*, shows our planet as a tiny blue marble with an ethereal cloud cover. Many credit the photograph, coupled with Rachel Carson's blockbuster publication six years earlier (Lawlor, 2012), as putting everyone on notice that the earth needed protection from its human population, thus providing the impetus for the global environmental movement.

Since that magnificent photographic moment, much has happened in the fight to protect the planet, from the creation of Earth Day in 1970 to the Paris Climate Accords. Climate change is real, although, a Pew Research Center survey (Funk and Kennedy, 2016) revealed that only 48 percent of adults in the United States believe climate change is caused by human activity, while 97 percent of actively publishing scientists believe so (see https://climate.nasa .gov/scientific-consensus/).

The survey also revealed that the more one knows about climate change, the more likely one is to understand the negative and costly impact humans have on the only planet in the known universe to sustain life as we understand it. Many notable nonfiction titles are available for young readers to gain an understanding of climate change and the havoc humans are reeking on the planet.

There are commendable picture book biographies about John Muir— considered the United States' first environmentalist/conservationist (Lasky, 2006)—and one high-energy picture book biography about Theodore Roosevelt, John Muir, and the creation of America's national parks (Rosenstock, 2012).

Everyone can help to maintain a healthy and safe environment through recycling. Almost anything can be recycled—all one has to do is follow the coding system found on the bottom of most containers. That numbering system, which is used globally, was created by Milly Zantow, an Oklahoma native who also pioneered plastic recycling (Moser, 2016). Plastic is a ubiquitous pollutant that, when discarded carelessly, can harm animals on land and

TEXTBOX 1.2

SOCIAL JUSTICE: CLIMATE CHANGE
AND OTHER ENVIRONMENTAL ISSUES

Climate Change

A warmer world: From polar bears to butterflies, how climate change affects wildlife (Arnold, 2012)

How we know what we know about our changing climate: Scientists and kids explore global warming (Cherry and Braasch, 2008)

Earth in the hot seat (Delano, 2009)

Energy island: How one community harnessed the wind and changed their world (Drummond, 2011)

Green city: How one community survived a tornado and rebuilt for a sustainable future (Drummond, 2016)

Pedal power: How one community became the bicycle capital of the world (Drummond, 2017)

It's getting hot in here: The past, present and future of climate change (Heos, 2016)

Why are the ice caps melting? The dangers of global warming (Rockwell, 2006)

Global warming (Simon, 2010)

Other Environmental Issues

Tracking trash: Flotsam, jetsam, and the science of ocean motion (Burns, 2007)

The hive detectives: Chronicle of a honey bee catastrophe (Burns, 2010)

John Muir: America's first environmentalist (Lasky, 2006)

The polar bear scientists (Lourie, 2012)

The case of the vanishing golden frogs: A scientific mystery (Markle, 2012)

Chasing cheetahs: The race to save Africa's fastest cat (Montgomery, 2014)

What Milly did: The remarkable pioneer of plastics recycling (Moser, 2016)

When the wolves returned: Restoring nature's balance in Yellowstone (Patent, 2008)

The call of the osprey (Patent, 2016)

One plastic bag: Isatou Ceesay and the recycling women of the Gambia (Paul, 2015)

The camping trip that changed America: Theodore Roosevelt, John Muir and our national parks (Rosenstock, 2012)

Parrots over Puerto Rico (Roth and Trumbore, 2013)

The buzz on bees: Why are they disappearing? (Rotner and Woodhall, 2010)

Gorilla doctors: Saving endangered great apes (Turner, 2005)

The frog scientist (Turner, 2009)

in the sea. When plastic bags became a problem in the Gambia, Isatou Ceesay formed a women's group to repurpose the bags (Paul, 2015). Plastic and other types of trash have become so prevalent in oceans that scientists study how the motion of the water moves the flotsam about (Burns, 2007).

Human encroachment on animal habitats increased world temperatures due to climate change, use of toxic pesticides, and thoughtless discarding of prescription drugs. These issues have placed a veritable Noah's ark of animals on the road to genetic anomalies and, in some cases, extinction of creatures such as frogs (Markel, 2012; Turner, 2009), polar bears (Lourie, 2012), honey bees (Burns, 2010; Rotner, 2010), and cheetahs (Montgomery, 2014). There also have been success stories, such as the gray wolf (Patent, 2008) and the osprey (Patent, 2015).

Nonviolent Acts of Civil Disobedience

People walking or marching (and on occasion, playing basketball) for freedom can be found throughout the annals of history. From the mid-nineteenth century until the passage of the Nineteenth Amendment in 1920, women suffragists marched (Bausum, 2004). In 1930, Gandhi led the Salt March to the sea as a nonviolent protest to British rule in India (McGinty, 2013). In 1944, an all-black college basketball team met in secret to play an all-white college basketball team.

There were rules against integrated play, but the black coach, John McClendon, thought little of those rules. The game he set up became the first integrated basketball game in the country. After the first game, the players integrated themselves, and two mixed teams played against each other (Coy, 2015). Thirty-three years after Gandhi led the Salt March, Dr. Martin Luther King Jr., a student of Gandhi's nonviolent civil protests, made one of the most famous speeches of his illustrious career at the 1963 March on Washington (Kelley, 2017).

By walking to work, the black citizens of Montgomery, Alabama, broke that city's segregated bus system (Freedman, 2006). Young people took to the streets for the 1963 Birmingham Children's Crusade (Levinson, 2012, 2017). There were marches for voting rights (Freedman, 2014; Partridge, 2009). James Meredith led a march, which many consider the line of demarcation between peaceful civil disobedience and more active protests by students—for example, Stokely Carmichael—who were tired of turning the other cheek (Bausum, 2017).

Civil disobedience was, and is, often fraught with violence, whereby those who were protesting were threatened, beaten, and even killed by the oppressors. Nazi Germany was a toxic environment that gave rise to many resistance movements. Members of these movements were always in danger and if caught were sentenced to death, often by beheading. The White Rose movement (Freedman, 2016) was started by Hans and Sophie Scholl—siblings who were early members of the Hitler Youth, became disillusioned with Hitler and his minions, and began distributing leaflets encouraging Germans to defy the Nazis.

Both were beheaded along with other members of the movement. Numerous citizens became members of resistance movements to protest and undermine the Nazi government. Some went so far as to plot the death of Hitler. One unlikely conspirator was Dietrich Bonhoeffer (McCormick, 2016), a dapper young man who was a pastor and spy. In Nazi Germany, civil disobedience took on the mantle of guerilla warfare. Doreen Rappaport's (2012) collective biography of partisans who were members of the Jewish resistance revealed the courage of those who used a multitude of tactics to undermine the Nazi regime.

Give me your tired, your poor. Poet Emma Lazarus's "The New Colossus" is inscribed on the pedestal of the Statue of Liberty. That poem and its oft-quoted lines have welcomed immigrants flocking to the United States since 1903. Lazarus was moved to write the sonnet to honor the plight of thousands of Eastern European Jews immigrating to this country to escape pogroms and other harsh conditions in their homelands (Glaser, 2010). Stories of immigration to the United States do not always give the true picture of the difficulties of immigration.

Ellis Island stories are well known in US immigration history (Peacock, 2007), but less is known about its West Coast equivalent—Angel Island—the port of entry for immigrants from China, Japan, and Korea (Freedman, 2014). The Chinese Exclusion Act made it particularly difficult for Chinese immigrants to enter the country. They were often kept on ships for weeks, even months at a time, trying to prove they were worthy of living in "Gold Mountain."

The Chinese were not the only immigrants to suffer in their attempts to enter the United States. In a stunning history of immigration in the United States, Bausum (2009) reveals a less than exemplary record of welcoming all immigrants. The St. Louis, a ship filled with Jewish refugees from Nazi Germany, was denied entry into the United States. Many of the refugees on board were returned to Nazi Germany, imprisoned, and then died in concentration camps. Also during World War II, Japanese Americans were detained in internment camps.

Emma Goldman had lived in the United States for thirty years before she was deported to Russia because she was deemed a dangerous extremist. In addition to these three cases (the St. Louis, Japanese Internment, Emma Goldman) Bausum highlights other instances when the United States did not welcome immigrants to its shores despite their being citizens here already. The only indigenous peoples (original and non-immigrant peoples) in this country are Native Americans—who, often to their detriment, allowed pioneers to settle in many areas with little or no fanfare.

TEXTBOX 1.3

SOCIAL JUSTICE: IMMIGRATION, VOTING RIGHTS, AND CIVIL RIGHTS FOR ALL

With courage and cloth: Winning the fight for a woman's right to vote (Bausum, 2004)

Denied, detained, deported: Stories from the dark side of American immigration (Bausum, 2009)

Stonewall: Breaking out in the fight for gay rights (Bausum, 2015)

The march against fear: The last great walk of the Civil Rights Movement and the emergence of Black Power (Bausum, 2017)

Game changer: John McClendon and the secret game (Coy, 2015)

Freedom walkers: The story of the Montgomery Bus Boycott (Freedman, 2006)

Angel Island: Gateway to Gold Mountain (Freedman, 2014)

*Because they marched: The people's campaign for voting rights that changed Americ*a (Freedman, 2014)

We've got a job: The 1963 Birmingham Children's March (Levinson, 2012)

The youngest marcher: The story of Audrey Faye Hendricks, a young civil rights activist (Levinson, 2017)

Marching for freedom: Walk together children and don't you grow weary (Partridge, 2009)

At Ellis Island: A history in many voices (Peacock, 2007)

Freedom summer: The 1964 struggle for civil rights in Mississippi (Rubin, 2014)

Brown v Board of Education: A fight for simple justice (Rubin, 2016)

Separate is never equal: Sylvia Mendez and her family's fight for desegregation (Tonatiuh, 2014)

FINAL THOUGHTS

Since the publication of Comenius's *Orbis Pictus*, nonfiction has played a vital role in helping children make sense of their world. Often called the genre of inquiry, nonfiction offers readers current information. Children can read about great white sharks (Montgomery, 2016), about the world's smartest birds—crows (Turner, 2016), or the destructive power of superstorms (Cherrix, 2017). These touchstone titles provide readers with in-depth exposure to one topic instead of snippets of information that are found in textbooks.

Textbooks are often outdated by the time they are published. Furthermore, they can be poorly written and filled with errors. Imagine the difficulties in elementary science classes the year Pluto was reclassified as a dwarf planet. A savvy teacher could select Scott's (2007) well-written book instead of using the required science textbook that was sent to press before Pluto's demotion to dwarf planet.

Biographies—picture book and otherwise—can introduce readers to individuals they would not typically read about in textbooks: for example, Vivien Thomas, whose innovative surgical technique saved hundreds of "blue babies." Jim Crow laws prevented Thomas, an African American, from receiving recognition for his work. The two white doctors who had to have Thomas in the operating rooms with them to know how to use his technique received credit for developing it. Thomas's name was nowhere to be found (Hooks, 2016; Murphy, 2015). It took almost three decades for Thomas to receive the national recognition for the technique he had perfected.

The best examples of nonfiction contain stunning photography or illustrations, well-researched subject matter, and excellent wordsmithing—attributes that attract readers of all ages who want to know about real things and people—real facts—the antidote for fake news and questionable truths.

REFERENCES

Bader, B. (2013). "Persons of interest: The untold rewards of picture book biographies." *Horn Book Magazine*, 89(5), 11–18. Retrieved from *Omni Fulltext Mega (H.W. Wilson)*.

Brown, D. (2007). "Sifting through the details: Writing biographies for children." *Language Arts* 84(6), 549–51. (print)

Carter, B. (2003). "Reviewing biography." *Horn Book Magazine*, 79, 165–74. Retrieved from *Academic Search Premier*.

Duthie, C. (1998). "It's just plain real! Introducing young children to biography and autobiography." *The New Advocate* 11(3), 219–27. (print)

Freedman, R. (1994). "Bring 'em back alive: Writing history and biography for young people." *School Library Journal* 40, 138–41. Retrieved from *Omni Fulltext Mega (H.W. Wilson)*.

Funk, C., and Kennedy, B. (2016, October 4). Pew Research Center: The politics of climate. Accessed April 7, 2018. http://www.pewinternet.org/2016/10/04/the-politics-of-climate/.

Giblin, J. C. (2000). "More than the facts: A hundred years of children's nonfiction." *Horn Book Magazine*, 76 (4), 413–24. (print)

Kluger, J. (2013, December 24). Earthrise on Christmas Eve: The picture that changed the world. *Time On-line*. Accessed April 7, 2018. http://science.time.com/2013/12/24/earthrise-on-christmas-eve-the-picture-that-changed-the-world/.

Lawlor, L. (2012). *Rachel Carson and her book that changed the world*. Illustrated by L. Beingessner. New York: Holiday House.

Moore, A.W. (1985). "A question of accuracy: Errors in children's biographies." *School Library Journal*, 45, 34–35.

Rosen, J. (2013, October). Publishers respond to Common Core. *Publishers Weekly, 260* (43), 26–28. Retrieved from *Omni Fulltext Mega (H.W. Wilson)* Accessed: April 6, 2018.

Sanderson, P. (2004). "True tales: From bee behavior to the life of Buddha, not all comics are fiction." *School Library Journal*, 50(8), 14-19. Retrieved from *Omni Fulltext Mega (H.W. Wilson).*

Scientific consensus: Earth's climate is warming (n.d.). Accessed June 22, 2017. https://climate.nasa.gov/scientific-consensus/.

Sidman, J. (2016). *Before morning*. Illustrated by B. Krommes. Boston: Houghton Mifflin Harcourt.

CHILDREN'S BOOKS CITED

Bausum, A. (2004). *With courage and cloth: Winning the fight for a woman's right to vote*. Washington, DC: National Geographic.

———. (2009). *Denied, detained, deported: Stories from the dark side of American immigration*. Washington, DC: National Geographic.

———. (2017). *The march against fear: The last great walk of the Civil Rights Movement and the emergence of Black Power*. Washington: DC: National Geographic.

Brown, D. (2013). *The Great American Dustbowl*. Boston: Houghton Mifflin.

———. (2015). *Drowned city: Hurricane Katrina and New Orleans*. Boston: Houghton Mifflin Harcourt.

Bryan, A. (2016). *Freedom over me: Eleven slaves, their lives and dreams brought to life by Ashley Bryan*. New York: Atheneum.

Burleigh, R. (2016). *Solving the puzzle under the sea: Marie Tharp maps the ocean floor*. New York: Simon & Schuster.

Burns, L. G. (2007). *Tracking trash: Flotsam, jetsam, and the science of ocean motion*. Boston: Houghton Mifflin.

———. (2010). *The hive detectives: Chronicle of a honey bee catastrophe*. Boston: Houghton Mifflin.

Cherrix, A. (2017). *Eye of the storm: NASA, drones and the race to crack the hurricane code.* Boston: Houghton Mifflin Harcourt.

Colman, P. (2002). *Where the action was: Women war correspondents in World War II*. New York: Crown.

Cooper, I. (2014). *A woman in the House (and the Senate)*. New York: Abrams.

Coy, J. (2015). *Game changer: John McClendon and the secret game*. Minneapolis, MN: Carolrhoda.

Engle, M. (2006). *The poet slave of Cuba: A biography of Juan Francisco Manzano*. New York: Henry Holt.

Farrell, M. C. (2014). *Pure grit: How American World War II nurses survived battle and prison camp in the Pacific*. New York: Abrams.

Freedman, R. (2006). *Freedom walkers: The story of the Montgomery bus boycott*. New York: Holiday House.

———. (2014). *Angel Island: Gateway to Gold Mountain*. New York: Clarion.

———. (2014). *Because they marched: The people's campaign for voting rights that changed America*. New York: Holiday House.

———. (2016). *We will not be silent: The White Rose student resistance movement that defied Adolf Hitler*. New York: Clarion.

Glaser, L. (2010). *Emma's poem: The voice of the Statue of Liberty*. Boston: Houghton Mifflin.

Gourley, C. (2007). *War, women, and the news*. New York: Atheneum.

Hansen, J. (2004). *African princesses*. New York: Hyperion.

Harness, C. (2004). *Rabble rousers: 20 women who made a difference*. New York: Dutton.

Hooks, G. (2016). *Tiny stitches: The life of medical pioneer Vivien Thomas*. New York: Lee & Low.

Kanefield, T. (2014). *The girl from the Tarpaper School: Barbara Rose Johns and the advent of the Civil Rights Movement*. New York: Abrams.

Kelley, K. (2017). *Martin's dream day*. New York: Atheneum.

Krull, K. (2010). *Lives of the pirates: Swashbucklers, scoundrels (Neighbors beware!)*. Boston: Harcourt Houghton Mifflin.

Lang, H. (2016). *Swimming with the sharks: The daring discoveries of Eugenia Clark*. Morton Grove, IL: Albert Whitman.

Lasky, K. (2006). *John Muir: America's first environmentalist*. Cambridge, MA: Candlewick.

Lawlor, L. (2017). *Super women: Six scientists who changed the world*. New York: Holiday House.

Levinson, C. (2012). *We've got a job: The 1963 Birmingham Children's March*. Atlanta, GA: Peachtree.

———. (2017). *The youngest marcher: The story of Audrey Faye Hendricks, a young civil rights activist*. New York: Atheneum.

Lewis, J. P. (2014). *Harlem Hellfighters*. Mankato, MN: Creative Editions.

Lewis, J. & Aydin, A. (2013). *March: Book one*. Marietta, GA: Top Shelf Productions.

———. (2015). *March: Book two*. Marietta, GA: Top Shelf Productions.

———. (2016). *March: Book three*. Marietta, GA: Top Shelf Productions.

Lourie, P. (2012). *The polar bear scientists*. Boston: Houghton Mifflin.

Marsalis, W. (2005). *Jazz ABZ: An A to Z collection of jazz portraits*. Cambridge, MA: Candlewick.

McCormick, P. (2016). *The plot to kill Hitler: Dietrich Bonhoeffer: Pastor, spy, unlikely hero*. New York: Balzer + Bray.

McCully, E. A. (2014). *Ida M. Tarbell: The woman who challenged big business—and won!* New York: Clarion.

McGinty, A. B. (2013). *Gandhi: A march to the sea*. Las Vegas: Two Lions.

Montgomery, S. (2014). *Chasing cheetahs: The race to save Africa's fastest cat*. Boston: Houghton Mifflin Harcourt.

———. (2016). *The great white shark scientist*. Boston: Houghton Mifflin Harcourt.

Moser, E. (2016). *What Milly did: The remarkable pioneer of plastics recycling.* Toronto: Groundwood.

Moss, M. (2009). *Sky high: The true story of Maggie Gee.* New York: Tricycle Press.

Murphy, J. (2015). *Breakthrough! How three people saved "blue babies" and changed medicine forever.* New York: Clarion.

Nelson, K. (2013). *Nelson Mandela.* New York: Katherine Tegen Books.

Nelson, M. (2001). *Carver, a life in poems.* Honsdale, PA: Front Street.

———. (2005). *A wreath for Emmett Till.* Boston: Houghton Mifflin.

———. (2008). *The freedom business.* Honsdale, PA: Wordsong.

———. (2009). *Sweethearts of rhythm: The story of the greatest all-girl swing band in the world.* New York: Dial.

Partridge, E. (2009). *Marching for freedom: Walk together children and don't you grow weary.* New York: Viking.

Patent, D. H. (2008) *When the wolves returned: Restoring nature's balance in Yellowstone.* New York: Walker.

———. (2015). *The Call of the Osprey.* Boston: Houghton Mifflin Harcourt.

Paul, M. (2015). *One plastic bag: Isatou Ceesay and the recycling women of The Gambia.* Minneapolis, MN: Millbrook.

Peacock, L. (2007). *At Ellis Island: A history in many voices.* New York: Atheneum.

Powell, P. H. (2014). *Josephine: The dazzling life of Josephine Baker.* Illustrated by C. Robinson. San Francisco: Chronicle Books.

Rappaport, D. (2012). *Beyond courage: The untold story of the Jewish Resistance during the Holocaust.* Cambridge, MA: Candlewick.

Robinson, F. (2016). *Ada's ideas: The story of Ada Lovelace, the world's first computer programmer.* New York: Abrams.

Rosenstock, B. (2012). *The camping trip that changed America: Theodore Roosevelt, John Muir and our national parks.* New York: Dial.

Rotner, S. & Woodhall, A. (2010). *The buzz on bees: Why are they disappearing?* New York: Holiday House.

Scott, E. (2007). *When is a planet not a planet? The story of Pluto.* New York: Clarion.

Shange, N. (2009). *Coretta Scott.* New York: HarperCollins.

Smith, C. R., Jr. (2015). *28 days: Moments in black history that changed the world.* New York: Roaring Brook.

Stone, T. L. (2013). *Who said women can't be doctors?* New York: Henry Holt.

Thimmesh, C. (2009). *Lucy long ago: Uncovering the mystery of where we came from.* Boston: Houghton Mifflin.

Turner, P. S. (2009). *The frog scientist.* Boston: Houghton Mifflin.

———. (2016). *Crow smarts: Inside the brain of the world's brightest bird.* Boston: Houghton Mifflin Harcourt.

Weatherford, C. B. (2008). *I, Matthew Henson: Polar explorer.* New York: Walker.

———. (2015). *Voice of freedom: Fannie Lou Hamer, Spirit of the Civil Rights Movement.* Somerset, MA: Candlewick.

———. (2017). *The legendary Miss Lena Horne.* New York: Atheneum.

Woelfle, G. (2007). *Jeannette Rankin: Political pioneer.* Honsdale, PA: Calkins Creek.

Chapter Two

Picture Book Biographies as Mentor Texts

Lesley Colabucci and Vivian Yenika-Agbaw

Summer months are often one of Vivian's best seasons of the year, for she can make a few trips to New York City and participate in cultural events that often enable her to rethink her approach to literacy teaching and experiences. One site she visits often is the Marcus Garvey Park, considered "one of the oldest public squares in Manhattan . . . [and that] has served as a meeting place for neighbors, a front yard and playground for children" (http://www.east -harlem.com/parks_mg.htm).

There is always something going on at the park, educational and cultural experiences often connected with music—the heavy rhythmic beat that emanates from the African drums, which get some passersby dancing or stepping to the tune. Such an experience is meant to sensitize black children in Harlem to their cultural heritage.

The music evokes memories of Africa; the determined look on the drummers' faces offers another kind of hope for the young children in that neighborhood, which makes one want to know more about Marcus Garvey, the person for whom the park is named. If these co-authors are so interested in learning more about this person, the hope is that more children in East Harlem will take a similar interest in the histories of their neighborhood. One obvious path for children who are curious to learn more about Marcus Garvey, a great historic figure in our national and global society, is to read a picture book biography about him. And Mohamed's (2004) *A Man Called Garvey: The Life and Times of the Great Leader Marcus Garvey,* may be an interesting one to begin with.

Like most picture book biographies, it is short and centers on Garvey, the subject of the biography, so that young readers are able to negotiate meaning, some of which might reveal his pan-African philosophy and ideas about political leadership. Thus, from a simple picture book, a reader is able to learn a great deal about a segment of national and global histories, leaving the nonfiction text experience with more questions that may necessitate reading another book to seek further answers.

Biographies for children are written to inspire and motivate young readers. It is easy to see how biographies of leaders, heroes, artists, scientists, and inventors, etc. can serve as role models for young learners. However, these texts can also serve as models of writing, which young learners may use as a template for the early phase of their initial writing, with the hope that subsequently, they will develop their unique voices and styles as artists. This is the thrust of this chapter, which also celebrates picture book biographies for their potential as mentor texts.

BIOGRAPHIES IN PICTURE BOOK FORMATS

In essence, picture book biographies are stories of real people that appear in picture book format. Picture books featuring diverse voices constitute a unique trend educators currently see in the field of children's literature, having been overlooked by both the publishing industry and educators for a long time. But now, with an understanding of what biographies in picture book formats can do to enhance academic content learning for young children while engaging them in the creative thinking processes, this genre of books can no longer be ignored. To Bader (2013), "what picture book biographies can do, at their best, can be done no other way. The pictures rivet attention, convey emotion, imprint a moment, the words are malleable . . . [and are] not mere explanations" (p. 18). Thus, more educators are now embracing what a picture book biography might afford learners with different learning styles.

Picture book biography is an art form that utilizes a wide variety of narrative modes. It offers students a simultaneously aesthetic and efferent experience whereby they are entertained as they learn key and other interesting information about the individuals whose stories they encounter.

Additionally, picture book biographies afford students opportunities for critical thinking, requiring them to look closely at how the rhetorical devices incorporated in the verbal narrative, and the sign systems embedded in the visual texts, may manipulate aspects of the creative process to further the author/illustrator's agenda. In this way, it serves as a mentor text for students learning to write their own autobiographies, or the biography of someone they belive has contributed to changing their society for the better.

PICTURE BOOK BIOGRAPHIES AS MENTOR TEXTS

Dorfman and Cappelli (2007) believe that "a mentor text is a book that offers myriad possibilities for students" (p. 3) and that such texts "serve to show not just tell students how to write well" (p. 4). They do recommend that one should strive to connect with the book in some way. The practice of teaching with mentor texts is well established and has been embraced by educators at a range of levels. This approach to writing instruction works well across the curriculum and emphasizes the importance of text complexity. Furthermore, using mentor texts is an effective way to incorporate multiple sources and more informational text in the classroom. As Saunders and McMackin (2004) explain,

> Well-executed picture-book biographies contain fascinating accounts of people who have made a difference in our world; clear and concise, their texts are often chock-full of inviting leads, facile transitions, and memorable conclusions. When teachers analyze what authors have done to create notable leads, transitions, and conclusions, students will discover that these books can serve as exemplars to improve their own nonfiction writing. (p. 25)

Mentor texts that anchor a literacy curriculum informed by critical pedagogy help to transform learning in significant ways. First, they not only expose students to a particular writing style, but they also convey factual accounts like other nonfiction texts that can be the basis for further inquiry. Secondly, they can be used to learn about facets of society. Thus, they help in filling gaps in our knowledge about certain topics.

Thirdly, they serve as a model of expository writing. Immersion in expository texts can be an important part of critical literacy, since nonfiction "motivates students as they search for questions about their world" (Werderich, McGinty, and Rosenstock, 2013, p. 4). Fourthly, the artistic styles of the illustrations and artistic media used in creating the art open possibilities for more dialogue on the art principles that may have informed the visual image.

PICTURE BOOK BIOGRAPHY SELECTION

Picture book biographies occupy a unique space in the world of children's literature, but selecting titles that students connect with, and that work well for writing and other creative projects, requires careful thought. A few teachers with whom these co-authors have worked have approached the selection process by posing a set of questions, such as:

- How might studying biographies serve the learning and literacy needs of our learners?

- What kind of creative experience would work well with text sets?
- How might we involve students in the book selection process?
- What types of picture book biographies are best suited for an autobiographical writing assignment?
- Which ones may work best for a design thinking assignment?
- What is the basic purpose for using a mentor text for creative thinking assignments?
- How have we used some of these texts in our classrooms before? Or have we used any of these texts in our classroom before? If so, how did learners respond?
- Ascertaining that the autobiographical writing is a worthwhile project that can transform learners' experiences with literary texts (nonfiction or otherwise), and in picture book format, offering opportunities for learners to develop their voices and sharpen their literacy skills is enough motivation for educators of any grade level to embark on the project.

Since reading and writing are inextricably connected, the selection of quality text sets the stage for effective writing instruction. As Gallagher (2014) explains, "if we want our students to write persuasive arguments, interesting explanatory pieces, or captivating narratives, we need to have them read, analyze, and emulate persuasive arguments, interesting explanatory pieces, and captivating narratives" (p. 1). Yenika-Agbaw and Sychterz (2015) concur, adding that learners must also know why they are doing the assignments, understand the different genres/types of writing, and understand the purposes for writing.

To select books for any classroom event, it is always a good idea to begin with the American Library Association's Youth Media Awards, which honor the best of the best in children's literature. While the Robert F. Sibert award specifically honors nonfiction, several other awards often feature picture book biographies as well. These include the Coretta Scott King Award, the Caldecott award, the Pura Belpre Award, and the Stonewall Book Award. In addition, picture book biographies often appear on the Orbis Pictus Award list sponsored by the National Council of Teachers of English. Books explored in this chapter were selected to illustrate how mentor texts can assist learners in the creation of their own autobiographies, how the texts have garnered those awards, and how they celebrate people from across the globe.

From a critical stance, this chapter argues that regardless of whose picture book biography learners are exposed to, teachers can guide them to claim ownership by writing either their own autobiographies or biographies of individuals they believe have contributed to the overall good of society in significant ways. In so doing, a classroom of learners generates a diverse body of nonfiction texts that can further serve the classroom community. By using picture book

Table 2.1.

Some Picture Book Auto/Biographies across Themes (Possible Mentor Texts)

Topic	Subject and Book Title	Author	Copyright Date
Artists	**Jean Michel Basquait** Radiant Child: The Story of Young Artist, Jean Michel Basquait	Javaka Steptoe	2016
	Horace Pippin A Splash of Red: The Life and Art of Horace Pippin	Jen Bryant	2013
	Diego Rivera Diego Rivera: His World and Ours	Duncan Tonatiuh	2011
	Frida Kahlo Viva Frida	Yuyi Morales	2014
Innovative Women	**Temple Grandin** The Girl Who Thought in Pictures: The Story of Dr. Temple Grandin	Julia Finley Mosca	2017
	Ann Cole Lowe Fancy Party Gowns: The Story of Fashion Designer Ann Cole Lowe	Deborah Blumenthal	2017
	Ruth Bader Ginsburg I Dissent: Ruth Bader Ginsburg Makes Her Mark	Debbie Levy	2016
	Emma Gatewood When Grandma Gatewood Took a Hike	Michelle Houts	2016
Inventors	**Thomas Edison** The Inventor's Secret: What Thomas Edison Told Henry Ford	Suzanne Slade	2015

(continued)

Table 2.1. *(Continued)*

Some Picture Book Auto/Biographies across Themes *(Possible Mentor Texts)*

Topic	Subject and Book Title	Author	Copyright Date
	Ben Franklin		
	Ben Franklin's Big Splash: The Mostly True Story of His First Invention	Barb Rosenstock	2014
	Mr. Ferris & His Wheel	Kathryn Gibbs Davis	2014
Inspirers	**Emmanuel Ofosu Yeboah**		
	Emmanuel's Dream: The True Story of Emmanuel Ofosu Yeboah	Laurie Ann Thompson	2015
	Muhammad Yunus		
	Twenty-two Cents: Muhammad Yunus and the Village Bank	Paula Yoo	2014
	Human Rights Champions		
	Dreams of Freedom	Amnesty International	2015
Scientists	**Marie Curie**		
	Marie Curie (Little People, Big Dreams)	Isabela Sanchez Vegara	2017
	Kamkwamba		
	The Boy Who Harnessed the Wind, Young Readers Edition	William Kamkwamba	2016
	Alexander Graham Bell		
	Listen Up!: Alexander Graham Bell's Talking Machine	Monica Kulling	2007

biographies as mentor texts, teachers then foster a kind of agency that situates students as creators of culturally situated texts that reflect their own personal histories and achievements as well as achievements of members of their diverse communities. See Table 2.1 for a short list of possible picture book biographies that can serve as a foundation for basic writing experiences.

This chapter focuses on the theme of innovative women, partly because we believe that women's contributions to societal development need to be made as visible as those of their male counterparts. Also, it is important to celebrate innovative thinking, and ways of looking at the world and of approaching what many may perceive as challenges. Innovative thinking is understood in this chapter as the ability to dare beyond one's comfort zone and do things from a novel perspective that pushes one's understanding of what is possible. The Oxford Dictionary considers an "innovative" person someone "introducing new ideas [one who is] original and creative" (https://en.oxforddictionaries.com/definition/innovative). The women whose biographies are considered here meet this criterion.

The four books (four books, three people) we use to demonstrate how picture book biographies can serve as mentor texts for a variety of writing genres include: *Who Says Women Can't Be Doctors?: The Story of Elizabeth Blackwell* (Stone, 2013); *Ada Lovelace, Poet of Science: The First Computer Programmer* (Stanley, 2016); *Ada's Ideas: The Story of Ada Lovelace, the World's First Computer Programmer* (Robinson, 2016); and *Solving the Puzzle Under the Sea: Marie Tharp Maps the Ocean Floor* (Burleigh, 2016). These are high-quality, award-winning picture books. Autobiographical writing based on these books as mentor texts should expose learners to a variety of narrative styles. To expand learners' engagement with these texts, they should apply a critical literacy lens, which helps them to delve deeper into issues.

As Flint and Laman (2012) found in their study of critical literacy in a writing workshop, this kind of writing has "seeds to larger social issues which are fodder for critical curricular inquiries" (p. 18). As students read and reflect on the hopes and challenges of those featured in picture book biographies, they are invited to reflect on their hopes and the challenges they face in their own lives.

INNOVATIVE WOMEN: MENTOR TEXTS FOR AUTOBIOGRAPHICAL WRITING

Biographies of pioneering and innovative women are on the rise. Stories of famous firsts, risky undertakings, and untold adventures have come to light through the format of picture book biographies. *Who Says Women Can't Be Doctors?* (Stone, 2013) is one such book, telling the story of the first female doctor. The narrative style in this book asks rhetorical questions of readers, engaging them in an imaginary and playful manner. Students can use a similar kind of questioning of the reader in their autobiographies. In addition, they can brainstorm events from their own lives and "sell" them as shocking or surprising using language from the text such as:

- "Well, you might find this hard to believe, but…,"
- "Some people actually…,"
- "They wondered what kind of girl she was. The kind of girl who…"

Like Elizabeth Blackwell, Ada Lovelace was an innovative pioneer who claimed a "first." In fact, the titles of the two books about Lovelace both note this: *Ada Lovelace, Poet of Science: The First Computer Programmer* (Stanley, 2016) and *Ada's Ideas: The Story of Ada Lovelace, the World's First Computer Programmer* (Robinson, 2016). However, the books are written in vastly different styles. As the books are read, teachers can have students closely examine the tone and perspective of each book. *Ada Lovelace, Poet of Science* begins with "Long, long ago, on a cold winter day, a lonely little girl…" while *Ada's Ideas* begins with "Once there was a girl named Ada who dreamed of making a steamed-powered flying horse" (unpaged). Students can begin their autobiographical writing picking from these two types of beginnings to start their own work.

In the opening paragraphs, both use the fairy-tale conventional opening that draws the reader into the story. This type of opening may seem different given the nature of the nonfiction genre; but its novelty makes it reader-friendly and presents a writerly style that may not seem so alienating to young learners. Students might work in pairs, with one interviewing the other and following the template to tell the story.

After writing the story following Robinson's or Stone's style, they could then switch drafts with other members of the class and have them illustrate these drafts mirroring the illustrators' art or making their own original decision as to how the art for their own autobiographies should look. They might also want to make decisions about the role of the illustrations: to confirm the story about a facet of their lives they are telling in the autobiography, or to expand the information of the written text. Their artistic styles, too, may vary from folk, cartoon, realistic, photography, and more; and likewise, their choice of media may vary. But they should be encouraged to keep a journal to reflect on the process, comparing their newly created auto/biographies to the picture book biographies of the mentor texts read.

Another trend in picture book biographies is the use of poetry as a format. One recent award-winning title about innovative women is *Voice of Freedom: Fannie Lou Hamer, Spirit of the Civil Rights Movement* (Weatherford, 2015). Each of the poems in *Voice of Freedom* could serve as a model for writing. For example, students can use "Delta Blues," which features the phrase "From sunup to sundown" as a template. This way of articulating the passage of time could be adapted for young writers with prompts such as:

- From yesterday to today
- From second grade to third grade
- From school to home
- From summer to fall

Young writers may also find biographies in a poetic genre a novel concept that offers an alternative way they can present information about themselves in their autobiographies or about someone they hold in high esteem in their biographical writings. Regardless of the templates they adopt for writings modeled after a mentor text, it is important that they publish their works in some way.

STUDENT PUBLISHING OF
PICTURE BOOK BIOGRAPHIES

There are a variety of ways that these can be published. First, the young writers can post their auto/biographies on the class bulletin board for all to see. If parents are encouraged to partner with the class, together as a community the written artifacts could be published through outlets such as http://studentreasures.com, which Vivian has used in the past to get teacher candidates' original stories published. These make great gifts to share with family members and friends. School Mate Publishing is another option to get the works of these young writers published (visit https://www.schoolmatepublishing.com). Other apps that may serve the same purpose include Flipsnack, Storybird, and ePudBud.

DESIGN THINKING AND MENTOR TEXTS

Design thinking is another approach to learning that affords students opportunities to problem solve in innovative ways. Thus, mentor texts not only serve as templates for students' auto/biographical writing, but they can also enable students to rethink aspects of the narratives, as presented in the picture book biography or autobiography format. Rabinowitz's (2014) *A Boy and a Jaguar* will be used here to illustrate this point.

Kwek (2011) remarks, "Design thinking is an approach to learning that focuses on developing children's creative confidence through hands-on projects that focus on empathy, promoting a bias toward action, encouraging ideation, and fostering active problem solving" (p. 4). So, from students' encounter with Rabinowitz's autobiography, they may gain a deeper understanding of what the problem might be and start thinking of creative solutions to a problem that is of interest to them.

Focusing on jaguars as an endangered species portrayed in the autobiography, the teacher then designs a unit on "The Preservation of an Endangered Species." In groups of four, young learners research a particular endangered species, such as hummingbirds (https://nationalzoo.si.edu/migratory-birds /hummingbirds); the types of hummingbirds that currently exist; where they are located across the world (http://ngm.nationalgeographic.com/2007/01 /hummingbirds/klesius-text); when they can be spotted in North America; how to spot them; their needs; and what might constitute a friendly habitat for them.

The teacher then arranges for a "birding tour" in a local zoo, or a field trip to Arizona (where hummingbirds are known to be found) to observe the birds in action, encouraging students to keep a journal on what they notice. On return, groups brainstorm ideas of possible solutions that might help save these birds from extinction, making a promise to the birds that is similar to the one young Allan makes to his animal friends in the mentor text. They work collaboratively to come up with a prototype of a friendly habitat that might keep these birds safe, and they share their idea with local conservationists for feedback.

At the end of the unit, they write a reflection on their experience. Design thinking follows a basic framework, as demonstrated in the Figure 2.1 flowchart from the Stanford d group:

Another version of this process follows this pattern, as explained at the web address that follows:

Understand—Observe—Point of View—Ideate—Prototype—Test

(https://stanford.edu/dept/SUSE/taking-design/presentations/Taking-design-to-school.pdf).

This is one way to get students actively engaged in the learning process—not only with the format of a mentor text and the expository writing genre, but also with the rich ideas that are embedded in texts.

Students become storytellers and truth makers sharing stories that offer possible solutions on how hummingbirds can be protected from extinction through different genres and formats, as well as informational and/or fictional stories

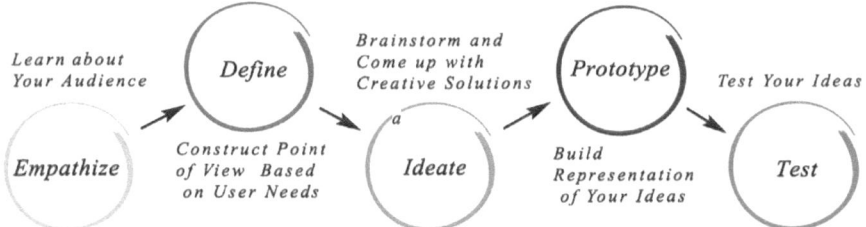

Figure 2.1. Design Thinking Process
Source: https://www.google.com/search?client=safari&rls=en&biw=1264&bih=756&tbm=isch&sa=1&q=D
esign+thinking+process&oq=Design+thinking+process&gs_l=psy-ab.3..0i67k1l2j0l2.1180137.1180678.
0.1183010.2.2.0.0.0.0.199.350.0j2.2.0.dummy_maps_web_fallback...0...1.1.64.psy-ab..0.2.350...0i13k
1.0.POmqPbZmj1k

about their trips to the zoo or elsewhere for their research. They tell "stories that connect" (Tofler, "Design Thinking") them with their environment and with each other, as they "learn, unlearn, and relearn" (Tofler, "Design Thinking"). And schools become places to innovate and not simply to consume knowledge.

As Kwek (2011) aptly concludes, "Schools whose curriculum and pedagogy fail to engage our younger generation as active learners and meaning creators are . . . not doing justice to a nation's development, especially when knowledge has become power in a globalized world" (p. 3). David Lee, an EdTech professional, has developed a YouTube video of design thinking in action in an elementary classroom, which can help teachers adopt this way of learning in their curriculum. See "Design Thinking with Elementary Students (1st Grade)" at https://www.youtube.com/watch?v=hvqST2ggvA0.

FINAL THOUGHTS

The picture book biographies featured in this chapter meet high standards for nonfiction. Some of the books in Table 2.1 can be considered multigenre because they are written in prose and poetry though they are in picture book format. All the books are ideal for re-reading and repeated sharing. Teachers should ensure that students are highly familiar with any text they will be using as a mentor text.

This type of close examination is essential to help "students become well versed in the particular genres, conventions and terminology valued by a discipline" (Pytash and Morgan, 2014, p. 10). It is of utmost importance that students "own" their writing, ideas, and creations, even if they do have to collaborate often in the process of innovating. While picture book biographies serve as models for this kind of storytelling, students need to know that the unique perspectives they bring to any kind of writing are key.

Narrative nonfiction of this nature has the potential to engage young readers in a more substantial and inspiring way than a traditional textbook approach. Also, books that feature diverse voices often appeal to students from a wide range of backgrounds, as they might be exposed to untold, neglected, or hidden stories that are unfamiliar to them. These books have the potential to empower young readers and nurture young writers to tell their own stories before they are forgotten or misrepresented. The books also have the capacity to develop students into creative thinkers and problem solvers. When utilized as mentor texts, these books can help students create, write, and retell in the most authentic, persuasive, and eloquent manner, thus cultivating a "can do" attitude!

REFERENCES

Bader, B. (2013). "Persons of Interest: The Untold Rewards of Picture Book Biographies." *Horn Book Magazine*, 89(5), 11–18.

Design Thinking for Communications Professionals. Accessed March 28, 2018. https://apps.prsa.org/Network/_includes/Storytell.pdf.

Dorfman, L. and Cappelli, R. (2007). *Mentor Text Teaching Writing through Children's Literature, K-6.* Stenhouse: Maine.

Flint S. A. and Laman, T. (2012). "Where Poems Hide: Finding Reflective, Critical Spaces Inside Writing Workshop." *Theory into Practice*, 51(1), 12–19.

Gallagher, Kelly (2014). "Making the Most of Mentor Texts." *Educational Leadership*, 71(7), 28–33.

"Hummingbirds." *National Geographic Magazine.* Accessed March 28, 2018. http://ngm.nationalgeographic.com/2007/01/hummingbirds/klesius-text.

Kwek, S. H. (2011). *Innovation in the Classroom: Design Thinking for 21st Century Learning* (Master's Thesis). Retrieved from https://web.stanford.edu/group/redlab/cgi-bin/materials/Kwek-Innovation%20In%20The%20Classroom.pdf.

Pytash, K. E., and Morgan, D. N. (2014). "Using Mentor Texts to Teach Writing in Science and Social Studies." *Reading Teacher*, 68(2), 93–102. doi:10.1002/trtr.1276.

Saunders, S., and McMackin, M. (2004). "Picture-Book Biographies as Writing Models." *Book Links*, 14(1), 25–27.

Taking Design Thinking to Schools. Accessed March 28, 2018. https://stanford.edu/dept/SUSE/taking-design/presentations/Taking-design-to-school.pdf.

Tofler, Alvin. Design Thinking with Elementary Students (1st Grade). Accessed March 28, 2018. https://www.youtube.com/watch?v=hvqST2ggvA0; EdTECH.org.

Werderich, D. E., McGinty, A. B., and Rosenstock, B. (2013). "Biographies in Focus: A Framework for Supporting Biographical Writing in the Classroom." *Illinois Reading Council Journal*, 42(1), 3–12.

Yenika-Agbaw, V., and Sychterz, T., eds. (2015). *Adolescents Rewrite Their Worlds.* Lanham, MD: Rowman & Littlefield.

CHILDREN'S LITERATURE CITED

Bryant, J. (2013). *A Splash of Red: The Life and Art of Horace Pippin.* Ill. by M. Sweet. New York: Knopf.

Burleigh, R. & Colon, R. (2016). *Solving the Puzzle Under the Sea: Marie Tharp Maps the Ocean Floor.* Simon & Schuster: New York.

Mohamed, P. (2004) *A Man Called Garvey: The Life and Times of the Great Leader Marcus Garvey.* Ill. by B. Braithwaite. Dover, MA: Majority Press.

Morales, Y. (2014). *Viva Frida.* New York: Roaring Brook Press.

Rabinowitz, A. (2014). *A Boy and a Jaguar.* Ill. by C. Chien. HMH Books for Young Readers: New York City.

Robinson, F. (2016). *Ada's Ideas: The Story of Ada Lovelace, the World's First Computer Programmer.* New York: Abrams Books for Young Readers.

Stanley, D. (2016). *Ada Lovelace, Poet of Science: The First Computer Programmer.* Ill. by J. Hartland. New York: Simon & Schuster Books for Young Readers.

Stone, T. L. (2013). *Who Says Women Can't Be Doctors? The Story of Elizabeth Blackwell.* Ill. by M. Priceman. New York: Henry Holt and Company.

Weatherford, C. B. (2015). *Voice of Freedom: Fannie Lou Hamer, Voice of the Civil Rights Movement.* Ill. by E. Holmes. Somerville, MA: Candlewick Press.

Chapter Three

Mirrors and Windows for All

Nonfiction Picture Books as Tools for Understanding Disabilities

Patricia A. Crawford and Kaybeth Calabria

"Where'd you get the books with us in them? I didn't know they were out there."

This question was expressed by a parent at an out-of-school reading program, attended by a diverse group of young children. Although the program was aimed at a number of different goals, the element that resonated the most with this parent was the knowledge that there were books "out there" with words and pictures that included representations of them and those who were dear to them; books that could be potential tools for their children to develop greater self-understanding, as well as ones that could help others understand the culture, world, and feelings that their children and family experienced on a daily basis.

This parent's heartfelt response speaks directly to Rudine Sims Bishop's (1990) concept of books as windows and mirrors; as texts that at once have reflective and illuminative qualities, that offer readers the invitation to see both themselves and others with greater clarity. Bishop's work is often used as a frame for highlighting the need for books that have racially and culturally diverse characters and themes. The need for literary windows and mirrors is also crucial for examining other areas of diversity, such as those surrounding issues of abilities and disabilities (Bishop, 2012; Blaska, 2004; Botelho and Rudman, 2009; Prater and Dyches, 2008; Smith-D'Arezzo, 2003).

The purpose of this chapter is to look closely at nonfiction picture books that have characters and themes related to disabilities. An overview of the nature of this literature is provided, along with suggested titles, innovative ideas for classroom use, and resources for further exploration.

CHILDREN'S LITERATURE AND
REPRESENTATIONS OF DISABILITIES

The representation of disabilities in children's literature has evolved over time. Historically, one of the greatest problems in this area had to do with omission; that is, there was a lack of inclusion in the pages of children's literature, with only a small number of books including stories of people who were disabled or providing attention to issues that surround different types of disabilities (Hughes, 2012).

When books, both fiction and nonfiction, did include stories of people with disabilities, the portrayals were often troubling, with depictions frequently presented in a stereotypical manner. Although authors may have intended that their depictions of disabilities would inspire empathy in readers, their portrayals often made people with disabilities seem to be worthy more of pity than of true affection and respect (Dowker, 2004; Wopperer, 2011).

The latter part of the twentieth century ushered in an era in which books for the young included a greater diversity of characters and in which sensitive personal circumstances and social issues were more often addressed in general. Accordingly, it became more common to find representations of people with disabilities in children's literature. While this presence is important, it is not enough. Critical readings indicate that in many of these books, representations of disabilities presented shallow portrayals, didactic storylines, or a paucity of accurate information (Beckett, Ellison, Barrett, and Shah, 2010; Wopperer, 2011).

Too often, literary depictions of people with disabilities continued to lack depth to ensure that readers developed the understanding that although coping with a disability might comprise a significant part of one's life, there are also many other facets to one's personhood, such as culture, family background, language, interests, and relationships (Ayala, 1999; Smith-D'Arezzo, 2003). This presentation of the whole person is crucial in the context of informational texts. In recent years, there has been an uptick of thoughtfully rendered representations of people with disabilities in informational texts such as memoirs, biographies, historical pieces, and guidebooks for understanding the nature of particular types of disabilities (Ayala, 1999; Prater and Dyches, 2008).

Since children's perspectives are impacted by the literature they read, there is a continued need for more thoughtful, well-developed, literary images of what it means to live with particular types of disabilities as well as what it means to be in relationships with others who might have these disabilities (McGrail and Rieger, 2016). There is also a need for related pedagogical resources and innovative strategies that will help children to think critically as they unpack the messages in disability-themed informational texts (Leland, Lewison, and

Harste, 2013). In order to meet these goals, it is important to keep in mind the nature of both efferent and aesthetic reading (Rosenblatt, 1994).

On one hand, this literature should accurately inform readers about the nature and implications of disabilities. On the other hand, transactions with these texts should offer an opportunity for readers to feel and resonate with the material encountered, so that they can develop informed, respectful, and empathetic perspectives about disabilities and the people who have them.

IDENTIFYING QUALITY LITERATURE

The Schneider Family Book Award provides an excellent starting place to encounter high-quality literature that "embodies an artistic expression of the disability experience" and that includes a "distinguished portrayal of people living with a disabling condition" (American Library Association, n.d.). Endowed in 2003 by Dr. Katherine Schneider and family, the award is given for books at three different levels: younger children, middle grades, and teens. Award winners can be fiction, biographical, or nonfiction and should portray the disability as "part of a character's full life, not the focus of life" (Schneider, 2014).

Excellent nonfiction picture books can be found among the Schneider Family Award winners, with biographies and memoirs of people with physical disabilities offering particularly rich touchstone texts for understanding the lives of real people who have lived with disabilities. For example, Jen Bryant's (2016) *Six Dots: A Story of Young Louis Braille* offers an elegant yet accessible up-close look at the pioneering young man who invented the Braille alphabet. Told from the perspective of young Louis, the book chronicles the wrenching story of how he lost his sight at age five:

"Where is the sun?" I cried.

But the sun did not come.

Words, illustrations, and the overall tone convey the challenges and depth of feeling that accompany Louis's situation. Yet these same devices are also used later in the book to show the rise of hope. The story line depicts Louis as a smart, determined, and clever boy who values education and sees the need for those who are blind to be able to read like everyone else. He is surrounded by loved ones who feel deeply for his situation. While some respond with pity, those closest to him provide tangible means of support.

Eventually, Louis develops the Braille alphabet, an empowering tool that enables those who are blind to communicate in reading and writing. His work transforms his own world as well as the worlds of uncountable others. This text offers readers a portrayal of Louis Braille as a whole person, one who experiences both triumphs and tragedy, who has demonstrated interests and ambitions in the midst of challenging circumstances.

Art Tatum was another man with a visual impairment whose life story is recorded in a Schneider Family Book Award–winning title, *Piano Starts Here: The Young Art Tatum* (Parker, 2008), a picture book biography told from a first-person point of view. Tatum's lifelong struggle with vision problems is situated within the broader context of his life as a person with a remarkable passion and talent for jazz music. Often regarded as one of the top piano players in the world, Art began his musical explorations at home, then in church and local venues. His growing reputation took him to many places, as he eventually turned his passion into a remarkable career.

This portrayal of Tatum's story is rich because it shows a life characterized by multiple dimensions. Art is a family member, a student, a musician. He is surrounded by a loving family, school personnel who encourage his talent, and caring friends with whom he engages in the everyday events of life. The printed text notes: "Denise and Janet, twin sisters who live next door, walk me to school every day now. They make sure I don't get lost or step in front of a street car" (Parker, 2008). Meanwhile, an accompanying illustration shows the three children joyfully walking arm-in-arm through the snow to school. In this book, the seriousness of Art's disability is never denied. However, it is socially situated as one component of a rich life, one that is deeply rooted with the people he loves.

Emmanuel's Dream: The True Story of Emmanuel Ofosu Yeboah (Thompson, 2015) is another Schneider Family Award winner that focuses on the impactful life story of a person who has a physical disability. When Emmanuel Ofosu was born in Ghana,

> Two bright eyes blinked in the light,
> Two healthy lungs let out a powerful cry, two tiny fists opened and closed,
> But only one strong leg kicked.

With these words, the author launches into the complex story of Emmanuel's childhood, a story of both hardship and hope. When his father sees Emmanuel's disability, he cannot bear it and leaves the family. His mother, however, has great faith and offers her son a steady diet of encouragement, high expectations, and tangible support, always believing that he can and will engage in activities that might seem impossible for someone with only one leg. With this support, Emmanuel engages in everyday activities, contributes to the household, and joins with the other children in school and games, even learning to play soccer and ride a bike.

When his mother dies, Emmanuel resolves to honor her "by showing everyone that being disabled does not mean being *un*able." Eventually, he garners support and devises a plan to bicycle across Ghana, raising awareness and hope for people with disabilities. In *Emmanuel's Dream*, readers will encounter a story that inspires and not mince words about the physical and emotional pain that often accompany having a disability.

While the above titles address important aspects of physical disabilities, it is also important for children to read books that introduce them to disabilities that are not as easily identifiable, such as ones associated with mental health. *Tuesday Tucks Me In* (Montalván and Witter, 2014) is an informational picture book that deals with this very topic, detailing the close relationship between Luis, a US Army captain, and his loyal service dog, Tuesday.

Told from Tuesday's perspective, the book provides a compassionate yet straightforward look at life with post-traumatic stress disorder: "Luis is a disabled veteran. He went to war and he came back home in so much pain that he couldn't live a normal life. So I do tasks for him" (Montalván and Witter, p. 9). Tuesday provides company and comfort as he helps Luis navigate anxious days, control his nightmares, and reach out to others by making school and hospital visits. Photos of Tuesday and Luis drive home the reality and currency of their lives, struggles, and relationship.

INVITING RESPONSE THROUGH INNOVATIVE PEDAGOGICAL STRATEGIES

Books like the ones described above seem to cry out for response on the part of readers. Issues related to disabilities are woven into the story line and are situated among a rich weave of facts, perspectives, and emotional pull. The disability is positioned as one part of a person's broader and fuller life circumstances. Since the books feature such complex issues, it is important that children have opportunities to discuss the reading, probe the content, and respond in meaningful and innovative ways. Activities such as the ones presented below can provide support.

"Getting to Know People" Activity

This activity offers a character mapping opportunity and a rich invitation to look closely and learn about people featured in the text. Thus, it is an ideal tool for working with memoirs and biographies. With careful framing, character mapping can help the reader situate the person featured in the text within a sociocultural context and bridge the reader's living and literary experiences.

Before sharing the book, the teacher might invite students to think about the following questions: *What does the person do and say? What does the person think and feel? What do others think about this person? What do* you *think about this person?* These types of critical questions allow students to think deeply about the text from a variety of perspectives: those of the central figure, those of others in the text, and their own. After reading the text with students, the teacher can then lead a discussion that scaffolds the character mapping activity. This can be done on chart paper as a collaborative group, as in the sample map in Figure 3.1, created from a discussion following a read aloud of *Emmanuel's Dream*. Or, the activity can be done individually or in small groups, as children complete a given template.

Students can then review the different thoughts and perspectives presented, and consider the whole life of the person depicted in the text. For example, students might conclude from this activity that Emmanuel is a smart and brave person who faced many obstacles. He biked across Ghana and showed that *disabled* did not mean *unable to do things.*

By using these types of character maps to find textual evidence, make inferences, and think critically by considering their own perspective as readers, children can grow in their understanding of both the complexity of human nature and the impact of sociocultural factors on the way that people and historical perspectives are presented in books.

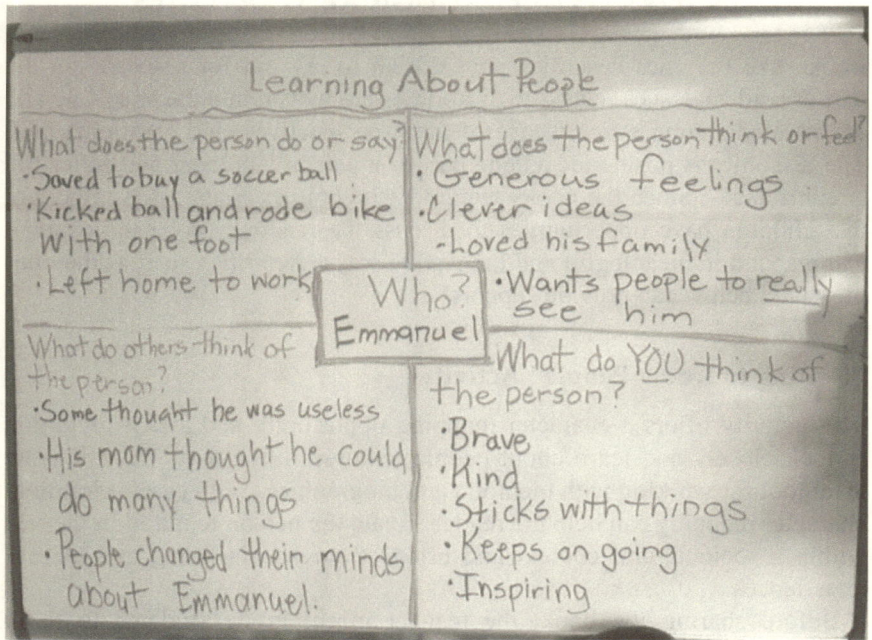

Figure 3.1.   Character Map for *Emmanuel's Dream*

Texts as Springboards for Going Deeper

Students might also respond to books that introduce issues related to disabilities by using them as springboards for going deeper into content. Children can take the knowledge gained as well as questions they have generated to probe the nature of different types of disabilities, and in turn consider ways in which they might learn more and take positive actions. Students can explore different multimodal sources to complement their learning from the picture book reading.

For example, several activities to further enhance the book *Six Dots: A Story of Young Louis Braille* can be found on the wonderful website created by the American Foundation for the Blind, http://braillebug.afb.org/. The information, activities, and games are designed to teach elementary children about why braille was invented, different ways to read and write braille, and the importance of braille for Helen Keller. Children can type in their names and see them translated to braille.

Other activities include seeing how background colors can provide a contrast to print so that individuals with low vision can better see the print on a computer monitor.

Students drawn to the life and work of Art Tatum can get a deeper sense of his amazing talent by listening to his music, which is available on numerous compact discs and YouTube clips. Those who want to learn more about the physical challenges encountered in *Emmanuel's Dream* may appreciate viewing live footage of Emmanuel's continued cycling and advocacy work (see https://www.youtube.com/watch?v=oOZm0ehCXp4).

Meanwhile, young children can learn more about service dogs like Tuesday by watching accessible, informational video clips such as a number of those produced by *Sesame Street* (see https://www.youtube.com/watch?v=aXTX88WKHaE as an example). Better yet, teachers and children might welcome a therapy dog into their classroom by arranging for a visit by someone from one of the service animal organizations available within many communities.

By tapping into multimodal and primary sources, young readers can go beyond the information presented in the focus texts and develop a stronger understanding of the people and circumstances at the center of their reading. They can become more knowledgeable, as they both think and feel with the lessons learned through these experiences.

"Everyone Is Welcome at Our School Photo or Video" Essays

The intent of these visual essays is to connect reading with real-life situations and help children recognize ways in which the environment can be welcoming to individuals with disabilities. The children and teacher can travel around the school looking for architectural principles of universal design that allow all individuals increased independence while navigating the school grounds. Pictures or videos can be taken of universal design principles such as curb cut-outs, ramps, specially marked parking spaces, braille signage, automatic doors, adaptive (lever-type) door handles, water fountains of differing heights, and wheelchair-accessible vehicles. Using a favorite presentation software, students can narrate the pictures or video and highlight these features that make it possible for individuals to navigate independently and to help an individual feel welcome at school, adding an element of praxis as the children take action to make their space more hospitable for all.

This spirit of welcome can be extended by role-playing ways to welcome students who may enter the classroom from resource rooms; by demonstrating ways to offer assistance and to interact helpfully and politely with students who have service dogs, use wheelchairs, or use a cane to navigate the school building. The following YouTube video from various agencies focusing on disability issues in North Dakota provides "10 Tips for Kids" on common social situations that can be eased by knowing disability etiquette: https://www.youtube.com/watch?v=-4kDbyiNihY.

As the narrator states, anyone could have a family member with a disability, know someone with a disability, or encounter someone with a disability; therefore, it is important to know how to meet and greet people properly and politely. Students can connect this learning back to the text by imagining that they are having a visit with the person about whom they have been reading. How might they greet this person? How might they change environmental factors to make the person they have encountered in the book feel welcome?

BOOK SELECTION

Nonfiction picture books provide a powerful starting place for readers to have vicarious literary encounters with disabilities and to look closely at the nature, nuances, and potential impact of these disabilities. Through conversation and guided learning experiences, readers can use the information and affective perspectives they gain to increase their understanding of others' disabilities, or in some cases, their own disabilities. There are many different types of nonfiction books related to disabilities that are appropriate for varied developmental and contextual needs among students, with concept books, biographies, memoirs, and varied forms of creative nonfiction numbered among them. (See Table 3.1 for additional recommended titles for the classroom.)

There are many resources available to educators who wish to choose and use literature containing disability-related themes. (See Textbox 3.1 for additional

Table 3.1. Recommended Books That Address Issues Related to Disabilities

Title	Synopses
A Boy and a Jaguar (Rabinowitz, 2014)*	This memoir recounts the author's struggle with stuttering and the frustration of not being able to express himself. The author learns to control his stuttering and uses his voice to speak out not only for himself, but also on behalf of wild animals who need protection.
Looking Out for Sarah (Lang, 2003)*	The true story of Sarah and her black labrador retriever unfolds. It exemplifies the powerful help that guide dogs can provide for people who are visually impaired and offers examples of appropriate ways children can interact with people and the guide dogs who assist them.
It's Okay to Be Different (Parr, 2001)	Appropriate for very young children, this book acknowledges and affirms many types of differences, including those related to ability and disability.
We Can Do It (Dwight, 2005)	Real-life photos and supporting text show children, each of whom has some type of disability, actively and happily engaged in a variety of activities.
Don't Call Me Special: A First Look at Disability (Thomas and Harker, 2002)	This straightforward introduction to the concept of disabilities shows that *everyone* has things they are good at and other things for which they need help. Provides an invitation for engagement in inclusive friendships.
Tic Talk: Living with Tourette Syndrome (Peters, 2007)	Told from the perspective of nine-year-old Dylan Peters, who has been living with Tourette Syndrome since age four. Dylan tells his story with insight, humor, emotional pull, and optimism.
I Can, Can You? (Pitzer, 2004)	This award-winning board book shows photos of babies and toddlers with Down syndrome who are happily engaged in life's daily activities. The text affirms what children can do and asks readers if they can do these things too.
Friends at School (Bunnett, 2006)	Presents a photo essay with positive images of an inclusive group of young children working and playing together.

Indicates a winner of the Schneider Family Book Award.

TEXTBOX 3.1

RESOURCES FOR ADDITIONAL CONSIDERATION

Beech, M. (2012). *Disability awareness through language arts and literacy.* Tallahassee, FL: Florida Disabilities Council. An excellent resource covering recommended literature, pedagogical tips, and suggested lesson plans for pre-k to elementary. Available at http://www.fddc.org/sites/default/files/file/publica tions/7%202%2012%20disability%20guide%20PDF%20final.pdf.

Derman-Sparks, L., and the ABC Task Force. (1989). *Anti-bias curriculum: Tools for empowering young children.* Washington, D.C.: National Association for the Education of Young Children. A classic resource for helping young children develop antibias perspectives. Suggested guidelines for reviewing books featuring people with disabilities are presented in an abbreviated form and available at http://www.libraryweb.org/images/NineWays.pdf.

Kids Quest is maintained by the Centers for Disease Control and Prevention (CDC) with information set up as a webquest. The webquests include information on the following health and disability issues: attention deficit-hyperactivity (ADHD), autism spectrum disorder (ASD), fetal alcohol syndrome, hearing loss, vision loss, mobility concerns, and Tourette Syndrome. The webquests appeal to fourth- to sixth-grade students; however, the facts, activities, suggested children's books, and stories about individuals with disabilities are informative for adults and can be adapted for younger students. https://www.cdc.gov /ncbddd/kids/index.html.

Center for Parent Information and Resources provides detailed information on infants, toddlers, children, and youth with disabilities. This website was produced under the U.S. Department of Education, Office of Special Education Programs. The following is a link to a resource that includes fact sheets on particular disabilities as well as categories of disability under IDEA law: http:// www.parentcenterhub.org/disability-landing/.

Arthur's Communication Adventure is part of a PBS site featuring Arthur the Aardvark from Marc Brown's popular series of books. The aim is to help all children understand how some children with visual and hearing impairments communicate and socialize with others. Suggested lesson plans supplemented with online and paper activities invite children to explore the use of braille and sign language, among other topics. http://www.pbs.org/parents/arthur/lesson /communication/index.html.

resources.) General guidelines about choosing antibias books are helpful in this regard, as are more specific suggestions that focus particularly on selecting books about disabilities. In general, it is helpful to review books with attention to the following:

Quality of the text: Does the book contain high-quality writing and appropriate, well-designed, respectfully rendered visuals? Is the book enjoyable to read?

Accuracy of information: Does the book convey sound, reliable information that is consistent with the reality of a disability?

Positioning of people in the book: How are people with disabilities situated within the story line? Do they have key roles, significant relationships, and a life in which the disability plays a part, but is not the totality of their experience?

Language: Is the language appropriate and respectful? Does it emphasize the person before the disability? Are hurtful and inappropriate words (e.g., crippled, weak, frail, pitiful, retarded, etc.) used? (Adapted from Konrad, Helf, and Itoi, 2007; Derman-Sparks and the ABC Task Force, 1989; Prater and Dyches, 2008)

FINAL THOUGHTS

Young readers need to see themselves and others with whom they engage in the pages of picture books. Those who love children and their books must be able to critically evaluate and respond to nonfiction texts with disability-related themes, and be able to utilize innovative pedagogical strategies to guide young readers to do the same. Ideally, these literary encounters have the potential to not only help readers learn about disabilities, but also to increase social acceptance for all and provide children with the tools they need to develop truly inclusive perspectives and relationships.

REFERENCES

American Library Association. (n.d.). *Schneider family book award.* Accessed: March 29, 2018. http://www.ala.org/awardsgrants/schneider-family-book-award.

Ayala, E. C. (1999). "'Poor little things' and 'brave little souls': The portrayal of individuals with disabilities in children's literature." *Reading Research and Instruction, 39,* 103–17.

Beckett, A., Ellison, N., Barrett, S., and Shah, S. (2010). "'Away with the fairies?' Disability within primary-age children's literature." *Disability & Society, 25,* 373–86.

Bishop, R. S. (1990). "Mirrors, windows, and sliding glass doors." *Perspectives*, 6(3), ix–xi.

———. (2012). "Reflections on the development of African American children's literature." *Journal of Children's Literature*, 38, 5–13.

Blaska, J. K. (2004). "Children's literature that includes characters with disabilities or illness." *Disabilities Studies Quarterly*, 24(1). Accessed: March 29, 2018. http://dsq-sds.org/article/view/854/1029.

Botelho, M. J., and Rudman, R. S. (2009). *Critical analysis of children's literature: Mirrors, windows, and doors.* New York: Routledge.

Derman-Sparks and the ABC Task Force. (1989). *The anti-bias curriculum: Tools for empowering young children.* Washington, DC: National Association for the Education of Young Children.

Dowker, A. (2004). "The treatment of disability in 19th and early 20th century children's literature." *Disabilities Studies Quarterly*, 24(1). Accessed: March 29, 2018. http://dsq-sds.org/article/view/843/1018.

Hughes, C. (2012). "Seeing blindness in children's picture books." *Journal of Literary & Cultural Disability Studies*, 6, 35–51.

Konrad, M., Helf, S., and Itoi, M. (2007). "More bang for the book: Using children's literature to promote self-determination and literacy skills." *Teaching Exceptional Children*, 40(1), 64–71.

Leland, C., Lewison, M., and Harste, J. (2013). *Teaching children's literature: It's critical.* New York: Routledge.

McGrail, E., and Rieger, A. (2016). "Increasing understanding and social acceptance of individuals with disabilities through exploration of comics literature." *Childhood Education*, 92, 36–49.

Prater, M. A., and Dyches, T. T. (2008). *Teaching about disabilities through children's literature.* Westport, CT: Libraries Unlimited.

Rosenblatt, L. (1994). *The reader, the text, the poem: Transactional theory of the literary work.* Carbondale, IL: Southern Illinois University Press.

Schneider, K. (2014). Foreword. *Schneider family book award manual.* http://www.ala.org/aboutala/sites/ala.org.aboutala/files/content/schneiderawardmanual-2-2.pdf.

Smith-D'Arezzo, W. M. (2003). "Diversity in children's literature: Not just a black and white issue." *Children's Literature in Education*, 34, 75–94.

Tschida, C. M., Ryan, C. L., and Ticknor, A. S. (2014). "Building on windows and mirrors: Encouraging the disruption of 'single stories' through children's literature." *Journal of Children's Literature*, 40, 28–39.

Wopperer, E. (2011). "Inclusive literature in the library and the classroom." *Knowledge Quest*, 39(3), 26–34.

CHILDREN'S LITERATURE CITED

Bryant, J. (2016). *Six dots: A story of young Louis Braille.* Illus. by B. Kulikov. New York: Knopf.

Bunnett, R. (2006). *Friends at school.* Cambridge, MA: Star Bright.

Dwight, L. (2005). *We can do it.* Cambridge, MA: Star Bright.

Lang, G. (2003). *Looking out for Sarah.* Watertown, MA: Charlesbridge.

Montalván, L. C., and Witter, B. (2014). *Tuesday tucks me in.* Photographs by D. Dion. New York: Roaring Brook Press.

Parker, R. A. (2008). *Piano starts here: The young Art Tatum.* New York: Schwartz & Wade.

Parr, T. (2001). *It's okay to be different.* New York: Little, Brown.

Peters, D. (2007). *Tic Talk: Living with Tourette syndrome, a 9-year-old boy's story in his words.* Illus. by Z. Wendland and K. T. Miller. Chandler, AZ: Five Star.

Rabinowitz, A. (2014). *A boy and a jaguar.* Illus. by C. Chien. New York: Houghton Mifflin.

Thomas, P., and Harker, L. (2002). *Don't call me special: A first look at disability.* Hauppauge, NY: Barron's Educational Series.

Thompson, L. A. (2015). *Emmanuel's dream: The true story of Emmanuel Ofosu Yeboah.* New York: Schwartz & Wade.

Chapter Four

Challenging Gifted and Talented Readers with Nonfiction Texts

Margot Dickey and Laura Anne Hudock

Rarely does a classroom phone ring with a parent on the other end of the line waiting to thank his child's teacher for the impromptu philosophical conversation he just had with his daughter, Layla.[1] As a former advanced academic resource teacher at a Title I elementary school in Fairfax County, Virginia, Margot received such a call. Earlier that day her fourth-grade students had been analyzing primary and secondary source documents that cite excerpts of the Code of Hammurabi in preparation for talking in a Socratic circle with classmates—an instructional practice that values authentic student interactions with any text on any topic through dialectic conversation.

Borrowing from the Socratic method, these fourth graders had been learning to critically engage with nonfiction texts on various topics through the generation of thought-provoking questions that amplify their perspectives and opportune authentic responses during conversation in the round (Copeland, 2005; Styslinger et al., 2010). The ensuing student-led discussion about translations of Hammurabi's stele carvings, though centuries old, had piqued Layla's curiosity about the notion of justice in ancient Mesopotamia.

Her inquisitiveness extended beyond the walls of the classroom. While riding as a passenger in her father's car after school, she overheard a National Public Radio broadcast about the denial of legal objections to an execution in Virginia. Given her earlier interaction with this Babylonian codification of laws regarding crime and punishment, Layla began to question aloud the grounds for clemency given the details of this death penalty case. Her father, a professor of ethics and religion at a local university, shared his astonishment over the phone with Margot. He had never imagined a conversation of that depth and complexity with his nine-year-old child.

Layla's unscripted inquiry needn't be an anomaly when teaching elementary-age readers who have been formally or informally identified as gifted and talented. As a facilitator, or as Paley (1986) suggests, the provider of "the glue" needed for "constructing a paper chain of magical imaginings mixed with some solid facts" (p. 123), Margot's instructional practice foregrounded this fourth grader's voice so that Layla might intuit her own logical connections, discoveries, and reasoned opinions. Pairing nonfiction texts with the pedagogy of gifted education has the potential to further encourage and develop critical nonfiction readers, so their articulation of spontaneous interconnections and self-realized insights may bloom in plenty.

Years later, in her capacity as an elementary educational specialist in the Advanced Academic Programs' district office—in which she oversees curricular design and implementation, leads professional development training seminars, and supports more than 120 advanced academic resource teachers—Margot reflected on this phone call. She wondered how this pairing might occasion pedagogical recommendations that help practitioners facilitate inquiry-based learning, especially in classrooms that serve economically disadvantaged and/or racially, ethnically, and linguistically underrepresented student populations (Ford, Coleman, and Davis, 2014; Passow and Frasier, 1996).

In their collective experiences, Margot and Laura—a veteran first-grade teacher, current undergraduate language and literacy education instructor, and doctoral candidate—frequently bear witness to the paucity of reading course content for general education teachers and acquisition of add-on certifications that focus on specialized, differentiated instructional strategies for challenging nonfiction readers who exhibit characteristics of giftedness.

To embrace differentiation is to help each gifted and talented reader effectively reach his or her potential in heterogeneous general education classrooms that are responsive to an individual's varied learning and socioemotional needs (Tomlinson quoted in Wu, 2013). While differentiated instruction has become a common practice for struggling readers, research findings suggest gifted and talented readers' particular needs are often overlooked (Reis et al., 2004).

When considering differentiation in the context of nonfiction reading instruction, an official school designation of student giftedness is unnecessary. Rather, informal teacher identification of a nonfiction reader's untapped gifted and talent potential may also prompt implementation of these specific learning strategies.

To these ends, Margot and Laura have culled the abundance of available research and reflected on prior classroom experiences. This chapter marries theory and practice to anecdotally describe several key characteristics that diverse gifted and talented elementary-age nonfiction readers exhibit and the corresponding instructional strategies that foster differentiated learning experiences.

IDENTIFYING GIFTED AND
TALENTED NONFICTION READERS

Reliance on unidimensional paradigms, namely psychometric measures that reify intelligence or academic aptitudes as definitive qualifications for gifted and talented curricular programs, fails to consider elementary-age readers' unlimited motivations, interests, and linguistic or creative talents. Criticisms of these test-driven measurements of giftedness cite the underrepresentation of culturally diverse or economically disadvantaged populations with potential for talent development (Passow and Frasier, 1996).

Notwithstanding school district policies that often codify the numerous research-based definitions of gifted and talented readers as criteria for identification (Jackson, 1988; Reis et al., 2004), many teachers' direct observations take notice of the uniqueness and cultural situatedness of each child reader that factor into curricular and placement decisions.

With the leveling of texts and readers that has been adopted in school districts and classrooms nationwide, reading at least two or more grade levels above the expected reading level of a student's chronological grade placement routinely marks a starting point for identification of gifted and talented readers. But this pedagogical adherence to a "simple view" of reading (R) as language comprehension (Gough and Tunmer, 1986)—a multiplicative relationship between accurately decoding (D) strings of letters fluently into words from which to signify comprehensible meaning (C)—or $R = D \times C$ potentially relegates literacy to incremental skill acquisition and quells readers' background experiences, prior cultural knowledge, and talents that may fall outside this formula (Street, 2003).

Gifted and talented readers may have perceived areas of weakness that fall short of this leveled marker, making self-aware declarations such as "I'm not good at reading X, but I'm better at Y." Two fifth grade students at a Title I school formally identified to receive gifted services, Ali and Adam (an advanced English language learner reaching proficiency), had failed state-mandated reading assessments for two consecutive years. In the months prior to their yearly grade-level testing and because of their previous test scores, school administration and reading coaches had designated them as candidates for reading remediation.

Conferencing with this duo for these purposes, Margot prompted them to self-identify any perceived areas of weakness during initial pull-out sessions.

Right away, they noted personal struggles in determining importance in non-fiction passages and understanding nonfiction-specific comprehension test questions. Instead of repeating prior teachers' past instructional attempts to improve on their strategies related to close reading, test-taking, and question analysis by reading generic nonfiction passages, Margot put aside the available leveled texts to which Ali and Adam had become indifferent.

Renowned British literacy theorist Margaret Meek (1995) urges practitioners to better understand children's responses to nonfiction texts. She remarks, "We need critics who are prepared to judge the nature and quality of the engagement required by the nonfiction offered" (p. 82). In looking beyond the convenience of standardized test scores that prescribe one-size-fits-all reading outcomes, Margot observed these fifth graders' waning confidences about their general reading abilities and objections to the emphasis on standardized reading tests as measures of school success. She keenly listened to them read their self-selected texts, noting enthusiasms, dislikes, and preferences.

This attentiveness informed her purposeful selection of excerpted quotes and passages about public education penned by Horace Mann, like those from the Library of Congress's online American Memory Collection, "An American Time Capsule: Three Centuries of Broadsides and Other Printed Ephemera," as the suggested nonfiction text. These fifth graders' active engagement in these readings and subsequent discussions validated their existing reading talents and eased their misgivings while fully addressing any stated weaknesses in reading nonfiction.

Anecdotal notes that reach beyond traditional reading assessments (e.g., Running Records) to focus on observed exceptional student behaviors outside of grade-level reading expectations serve many purposes. Such informal data collection aids Margot's curricular decision-making. This commentary evidence not only lends support to formal gifted and talented placement decisions that require completion of checklists for advanced thinking skills and behaviors, but it regards the quality of the individual student's engagement and nonfiction text selection too.

While acknowledging the divergency of giftedness definitions, educational psychologist Joseph Renzulli remarks, "no single criterion should be used to identify giftedness" (p. 83). Rather, he proposes, "persons who have achieved recognition because of their unique accomplishments and creative contributions possess a relatively well-defined set of three interlocking clusters of traits" (p. 83). Among his triadic clusters, "task commitment," Renzulli explains, "the ability to involve oneself totally in a problem or area for an extended period of time," attends to the characteristic passion, resolve, and assiduousness observed in gifted readers (p. 84).

With an idiomatic "nose in a book," young gifted and talented readers are often ahead of their peers and self-taught. Teachers may unintentionally overlook their unique needs to focus limited instructional time and attention on struggling readers. Consequently, stagnation potentially plagues these young gifted and talented readers' development, especially those in urban settings, as they lack optimally challenging opportunities to engage with nonfiction texts and experiences that promote self-regulation (Chall and Conrad, 1991; Reis and Boeve, 2009). Whether formal or informal, early identification of advanced ability generates documentation that apprises teachers' decisions about specialized instructional strategies to be implemented alongside nonfiction texts that likely impede occurrence of this plateau.

Research suggests that students who make their own text choices based on personal interests enjoy reading more (Reis et al., 2005). In a case study of upper elementary school-aged readers identified as gifted and talented, Leal and Moss (1999) note the following preferences when given the opportunity to select and engage in informational texts:

> 1) Unusual information and/or humor; 2) a depth of content coverage within a creative format; 3) intriguing information focused on capturing students' conceptual interest; 4) both efferent and aesthetic purposes; 5) mind-boggling details that stimulate the imagination; 6) accurate and appealing illustrations. (pp. 96–97)

To assist classroom teachers in understanding how Leal and Moss's (1999) findings may inform differentiated instruction, this chapter presents three easily discernible characteristics of giftedness that target these nonfiction preferences—voracious reading habits, heightened interests, and deep vocabulary use in self-chosen topics.

VORACIOUS READING HABITS

Some academically talented readers use nonfiction books to alleviate perceived boredom or to immerse themselves in conceptual topics of study. Kaleb, an elementary-age, gifted and talented student with bridging English as a second language proficiency, consumed more reading material than any student Margot had previously encountered. His head was tucked in a book during any and every free moment, even while traversing the hallways and ascending or descending the stairs. As soon as his school bus dropped him off, he stopped by the library to check out a stack of books. At dismissal, he'd return those books to check out new ones to bring home for the evening.

Concerned that Kaleb had been cursorily reading these books and wasting precious learning time, the school librarian approached Margot. In response, Margot invited her to observe Kaleb over the course of a day—to hear him turn pages and receive countless redirections to engage in classroom activities and conversations and see him actively contribute his learned knowledge. By the end of fifth grade he had read the entirety of the school library or very close to it! Kaleb epitomizes voracious reading habits.

HEIGHTENED INTERESTS IN SELF-CHOSEN TOPICS

Gifted and talented readers may self-select historical events or content-area topics to fervently explore and digest. Subsequently, they seek to amass and read as much material pertaining to the topic as possible. Two of Margot's former fourth-grade students, Clare and Quinn, shared a unique passion for World War II. Identified for full-time gifted services, both girls often swapped nonfiction book titles (see Textbox 4.1 for examples) and closely analyzed these compelling nonfiction titles.

They empathized with featured people, often female and of similar age, and easily voiced connections between treatment of marginalized groups

TEXTBOX 4.1

ELEMENTARY-AGE STUDENTS' SELF-SELECTED NONFICTION TITLES ABOUT WORLD WAR II

Jacobson, S., and Colón, E. (2010). *Anne Frank: The Anne Frank House authorized graphic biography.* New York: Hill & Wang.

Levine, K. (2016). *Hana's suitcase: The quest to solve a Holocaust mystery.* New York: Crown Books for Young Readers.

Leyson, L. (2013). *The boy on the wooden box: How the impossible became possible.* New York: Atheneum.

Rappaport, D. (2012). *Beyond courage: The untold story of Jewish resistance during the Holocaust.* Somerville, MA: Candlewick Press.

Samuels, C. (2013). *Life under occupation.* London: Hachette Children's Group.

during World War II and the post-9/11 "War on Terrorism." Given their intense focus on World War II, curated nonfiction texts such as the National Archives' online copy of Franklin D. Roosevelt's annotated draft of his "Day of Infamy" speech added primary sources to the girls' reading experience.

But not all their peers in this self-contained classroom were as enthusiastic and responsive to Clare and Quinn's self-chosen topic. Their preoccupation diverged from interests of age-level and ability-level peers who found the horrors of the Holocaust and the Blitz bombings of the United Kingdom macabre. Absorption in content markedly above their maturity level highlights a possible asynchrony in reading development—that is, their intellectual capacity for topical reading material exceeded emotional capacity for content.

Gifted readers' unique socioemotional needs may influence their responses to particular nonfiction text selections. Swayed by Clare and Quinn's overwhelming enthusiasm for this topic, a classmate, Kelsey, chose to read some of the selections listed in Textbox 4.1. In the days that followed, Kelsey's mother phoned Margot to voice concerns about her daughter's choice of reading materials and related exhibitions of anxiety (e.g., crying at bedtime and sleepless nights). Attuned to Kelsey's socioemotional needs, Margot suggested abandoning the topic and supplanted her self-selected nonfiction books with other ones that more appropriately matched her maturity level and personal interests.

DEEP VOCABULARY USE

As a third grader, Nolan struggled. He failed to complete any work, including readings of texts, in a timely manner. He withdrew from classroom activities. His desk and backpack were in constant disarray. He frequently exhibited behavioral outbursts. On paper, his county-mandated summative assessments indicated his ongoing failure to meet statewide mathematics and language arts benchmarks. Nolan's classroom co-teachers, comprised of general education and English speakers of other languages instructors, concentrated their collective instructional strategies on mitigating his deficits.

Meanwhile, Margot introduced a nonfiction book about dinosaurs, Rupert's (2008) *Dinosaurs in Action: Unearth the Secrets behind Dinosaur Fossils,* to Nolan's high-ability reading group. Like the flipping of a light switch, Nolan became animated. He actively participated and guided his peers through challenging pronunciations of species, time periods, and tools used by experts in the field.

Noticing a possible mistake in that nonfiction trade book—a dinosaur had been incorrectly identified—Nolan took it upon himself to collect research

from resources at home that confirmed his suspicions. His store of conceptual vocabulary knowledge far exceeded grade-level expectations. Hoping to
build on Nolan's confidence as a twice exceptional learner, his parents and
gifted resource teacher advocated for specialized instructional services to
capitalize on this spark in science-related content.

PAIRING NONFICTION TEXT AND
SPECIALIZED INSTRUCTIONAL STRATEGIES

Gifted readers' instructional needs typically exceed lessons that focus on
the differences between fiction and nonfiction texts and related features.
Incorporation of differentiated instructional practices apprised of identified
characteristics of giftedness and attentive to a student's nonfiction preferences supports reading development, not necessarily in terms of advancing
reading levels but, rather, metacognitive awareness of strategies to deeply
comprehend complex texts. The remainder of this chapter offers specialized
instructional strategies intended to promote gifted readers' critical thinking
about knowledge gleaned from nonfiction texts and applied to relevant problems or issues of choice.

DIVERSIFIED NONFICTION CONTENT AND FORMAT

Engaging gifted nonfiction readers through Project Based Learning (PBL)
authenticates nonfiction reading in the classroom setting through rigorous
and sustained inquiry. Buck Institute for Education (BIE, 2017b), a nonprofit
organization, explains PBL as "a teaching method in which students gain
knowledge and skills by working for an extended period of time to investi-
gate and respond to an authentic, engaging and complex question, problem,
or challenge" (n.p.). PBL motivates learners to engage in nonfiction texts in
real-world contexts. It values students' voices as they self-define their interests and choices in what work they produce (BIE, 2017b).

Projects begin with a carefully crafted and refined "Driving Question," that
is, an open-ended, engaging question "linked to the core focus of the project"
(BIE, 2017a). Though a PBL experience may be teacher-crafted to align with
curriculum, the Driving Question is typically generated from a real-world
context of relevance and importance to students. During this PBL process
students assume the role of an expert working in a specific field to produce
a public project in the likeness of that profession that wholly addresses the
Driving Question. Projects require research and readings to satisfy the "need

to know" information. Teachers may curate readings or aid students as they self-select texts to meet their research needs.

PBL has been central to Margot's Advanced Academic pedagogical practices. In 2015, the school context weighed heavily in her fifth-grade students' decision to initiate and actively pursue one particular project. Their new school, located on an urban campus—that is, a five-story office building—had been retrofitted to handle the capacity issues at the most populated elementary school in the Commonwealth of Virginia. Though aesthetically pleasing, the school lacked something of pivotal importance to all elementary-age students—a playground! Embracing a PBL approach, these students attempted to answer the following Driving Question: How can you, a designer working for the school district, create a playground that meets the district's specifications and the desires of the student population?

Given this localized problem, available nonfiction books in the school and classroom libraries were insufficient informational sources. Rather, purposeful connections to school and community stakeholders availed diversified nonfiction selections particular to this Driving Question.

Serving as an intermediary in the procurement of relevant resources, Margot arranged for these students to personally meet with the district specialist from facilities management and the existing playground vendor representative. She shared incoming emails and attached policy documents detailing the educational and accessibility specifications of equipment as well as catalogues from approved playground vendors. These students also read a featured news article on play and exercise from the *Washington Post* (Sohn, 2015). The architect for the school's renovation conducted a hands-on workshop on the topic of aesthetics, light, and design, bringing related brochures, storyboards, and flipbooks for the students to peruse.

After researching and collaborating on the types of playground equipment that best fit the design, play, and accessibility regulations, students created mock layouts to share and present to school and community stakeholders. Impressed with their high-quality work and deep learning, the school district later solicited student feedback on their final designs. The principal also deferred to these students' recommendations when budget and space constraints necessitated a choice between purchase and installation of equipment.

STUDENT-DRIVEN READING EXPERIENCES

Gifted readers typically begin each school year already surpassing grade-level benchmarks for comprehension, word analysis, and reading level. Even so, they often require instructional support in developing metacognitive awareness to monitor comprehension and adjust reading strategies as needed. Procedural transfer of self-regulated learning onto these gifted readers often vexes their teachers. According to Wilson and Bai's (2010) survey of pre-service teachers, pedagogical understanding may waver in "how, why, and under what conditions to use metacognitive teaching strategies" (p. 281).

Schoolwide Enrichment Model-Reading Framework (SEM-R; Reis, Fogarty, Eckert, and Muller, 2008), based on Renzulli's (1976) enrichment triad model—principles of differentiated instruction, consideration of students' individual nonfiction preferences, and metacognitive reading strategies—provides challenging learning experiences that foster self-regulation and fluency. Reis and Fogarty (2006) explain, "SEM-R includes three categories of reading instruction: (1) broad exposure to appropriate texts and areas of possible interest, (2) higher-order thinking skills training and methods instruction, and (3) opportunities to pursue self-selected activities" (p. 32).

The SEM-R framework gradually releases teacher responsibility for learning outcomes and social mediation of critical thinking onto gifted and talented readers. Shared thinking about nonfiction texts during read-alouds, reading conferences, or reading log debriefings help make metacognitive strategies visible to students. For more information about SEM-R, visit Renzulli Center for Creativity, Gifted Education, & Talent Development (Renzulli Center, n.d.b).

In her former self-contained, gifted third-grade classroom, implementation of the SEM-R framework enhanced Margot's reading instruction while motivating her students. During Phase 1, her teacher-directed "Book Hook" sessions piqued students' interest in nonfiction titles, authors, topics, or series (Reis and Fogarty, 2006; Renzulli Center, n.d.b; Reis et al., 2008).

For example, she read aloud biographies such as Bader's (2013) *Who Was Christopher Columbus?* with accompanying pauses to ponder higher-order thinking questions. Based on the Renzulli Center's (n.d.a) "SEM-R Implementation Resources," specifically elementary school bookmarks about point of view, Margot prompted her students to consider authorial bias in the presentation of limited perspectives. Students' subsequent deliberations extended to all nonfiction trade books on explorers, such as Juan Ponce de León and Jacques Cartier. See Textbox 4.2 for additional prompts and nonfiction book titles to possibly share with elementary students.

Phase 2 featured one-on-one conferences in which Margot carefully reviewed students' book selections as recorded on reading logs. As previously mentioned, Kaleb had a voracious appetite for reading. He listed prolific nonfiction titles he had read. Though he could regurgitate memorable facts in isolation, he blushed in silence when Margot prompted him to respond

TEXTBOX 4.2

ADDITIONAL PROMPTS AND
NONFICTION BOOK TITLES

Compare what you learned in reading *Brick by Brick* to what you already knew and/or thought you knew about the White House from reading Robert Sabuda's pop-up guide.

Sabuda, R. (2016). *The White House: A pop-up of our nation's home*. New York: Orchard Books.

Smith, C. R., Jr. (2012). *Brick by brick*. New York: HarperCollins.

How did an idea bring about change to a local community and/or globally?

Kamkwamba, W., and Mealer, B. (2015). *The boy who harnessed the wind*. New York: Dial Books for Young Readers.

Prévot, F., Fronty, A., and Clément, D. (2015). *Wangari Maathai: The woman who planted millions of trees*. Watertown, MA: Charlesbridge.

Rohmer, H. (2009). *Heroes of the environment: True stories of people who are helping to protect our planet*. San Francisco, CA: Chronicle Books.

Describe some science, technology, engineering, and/or mathematics jobs that might be related to this topic. What day-to-day work might such a professional do?

Bang, M., and Chisholm, P. (2014). *Buried sunlight: How fossil fuels have changed the earth*. New York: The Blue Sky Press.

Saujani, R. (2017). *Girls who code: Learn to code and change the world*. New York: Viking.

These "Book Hook" prompts are based on the Renzulli Center's online "SEM-R Implementation Resources" that include elementary bookmarks about nonfiction (n.d.a).

critically to his various nonfiction selections. Daily goal-setting related to the modeling of metacognitive reading strategies such as making intertextual connections and inferencing paved the way for Kaleb to advance his reading skills. See Table 4.1 for an overview of the student and teacher expectations in preparing for and conducting such a one-on-one conference.

Table 4.1.   One-on-One Conference Expectations

	Preparing for Conferences	*Holding Conferences*
Teacher	Select higher-level questions that support acquisition of skill(s)	Maintain warm and collaborative conference environment
	Employ conference rubric for criteria-based assessment	Bring assessment folio, SEM-R bookmarks, conference rubric
	Aim to confer with students weekly for optimal student growth and reflection	Model and support specific reading strategies
		Conferences should last no more than five minutes
Student	Complete reading log and assigned readings (self-assigned and teacher directed)	Bring book(s), other texts, and student reading log
	Reflective goal setting: consider what they need to be successful	Be prepared to read aloud, share ideas, and have conversations about reading materials

In Phase 3 students had the opportunity to helm their own reading experiences and inquiry projects using their newly practiced reading strategies. Virginia's Standards of Learning, namely social studies curriculum for third grade, highlights major contributions, architecture, and geography of several ancient civilizations. However, this overview failed to adequately quench Kaleb's thirst for more information. After tinkering with the "zoom in" feature on Google Earth, his inquisitiveness deliberated whether the founding of most major ancient civilizations occurred near rivers or large bodies of water. This connection inspired him and his peers to seek out additional information that might explain or confirm this queried assumption.

Kaleb's self-selected inquiry required a deeper dive into global awareness of nonfiction texts that seemed near impossible to broach during class time. So, rethinking how to maximize this scarce resource, that is, class time, for the benefit of her readers, Margot adopted a flipped classroom approach. Absent any definitive method for flipping a classroom (Bergmann and Sams, 2012, p.11), she catered to gifted and talented students' nonfiction preferences and educational needs.

Students controlled the path and pace of learning outside of the physical classroom environment through access to resources on blended learning platforms such as Google Classroom or Blackboard Learn. Margot facilitated the curation and posting of challenging nonfiction texts aligned with Kaleb's reading abilities and self-selected inquiry topic.

With an opportunity to read online articles from *National Geographic*, explore maps and photographs housed in museum collections—artifacts and paintings—and access traditional myths about deities representative of each ancient civilization under review, Kaleb actively engaged with these challenging multimodal resources at home. Each morning he entered the classroom eager to share his discoveries with peers, ask clarifying questions, or address any misconceptions about the reading materials. In this collaborative setting Kaleb worked to evidence or disprove his claim while furthering conceptual knowledge, as well as bolstering his metacognitive awareness and critical thinking skills during independent reading and response.

FINAL THOUGHTS

While early identification of a student's giftedness is vital to the progression of his or her critical readership of nonfiction and other texts, so, too, is differentiated instruction. Attentiveness to a student's nonfiction preferences and reading habits helps to inform adoption of instructional approaches that motivate, encourage problem-solving, and generate critical insights.

In this chapter's many anecdotes, Margot reflected on her role as facilitator of nonfiction reading experiences, the provider of the "glue" (Paley, 1986). She noted key characteristics of formally or informally identified gifted and talented readers that guided her orchestration of differentiated learning opportunities tailored to their specific needs and interests. She positioned them to critically engage with nonfiction readings, as they would other kinds of readings.

Content addressed in student-initiated inquiries may borrow from a wide variety and delivery of formats that afford gifted and talented readers—as well as other readers not officially labeled as such—challenging alternatives to library bound nonfiction books. As resources within the physical or virtual classroom environment, these nonfiction texts curated by students, teachers, or stakeholders in the greater school community lend authenticity. These nonfiction selections also incentivized students in their pursuits of self-driven reading experiences that exceeded typical grade-level expectations and extended their metacognitive awareness of reading strategies.

NOTE

1. All student names are pseudonyms.

REFERENCES

Bergmann, J., and Sams, A. (2012). *Flip your classroom: Reach every student in every class every day*. Eugene, OR: International Society for Technology in Education.

Buck Institute for Education. (2017a). Driving Question [Webinar]. Accessed April 2, 2018. http://www.bie.org/object/webinars_archived/driving_questions.

———. (2017b). What is PBL? Accessed April 6, 2018. http://www.bie.org/about/what_pbl.

Chall, J. S., and Conrad, S. S. (1991). *Should textbooks challenge students? The case for easier or harder books.* New York: Teachers College Press.

Copeland, M. (2005). *Socratic circles: Fostering critical and creative thinking in middle and high school*. Portland, ME: Stenhouse Publishers.

Ford, D. Y., Coleman, M. R., and Davis, J. L. (2014). "Racially, ethnically, and linguistically different gifted and talented students." *Gifted Child Today*, 37, 133–34.

Gough, P. B., and Tunmer, W. E. (1986). "Decoding, reading, and reading disability." *Remedial and Special Education*, 7, 6–10.

Jackson, N. E. (1988). Precocious reading ability: What does it mean? *Gifted Child Quarterly, 32*(1), 200–204.

Leal, D. & Moss, B. (1999). Encounters with information text: Perceptions and insights from four gifted readers. *Reading Horizons, 40*(2), 81–101.

Meek, M. (1995). *Information & book learning.* London: Thimble.

Paley, V. G. (1986). "On listening to what the children say." *Harvard Educational Review*, 56(2), 122–31.

Passow, A. H., and Frasier, M. M. (1996). "Toward improving identification of talent potential among minority and disadvantaged students." *Roeper Review*, 18(3), 198.

Reis, S. M., and Boeve, H. (2009). "How academically gifted elementary, urban students respond to challenge in an enriched, differentiated reading program." *Journal for the Education of the Gifted*, 33(2), 203–40. doi:10.1177/016235320903300204.

Reis, S. M., Eckert, R. D., Jacobs, J., Coyne, M., Richards, S. Briggs, C. J., Schreiber, F. J., & Gubbins, E. J. (2005*). The schoolwide enrichment model-Reading framework*. Storrs: University of Connecticut, The National Research Center on the Gifted and Talented.

Reis, S. M., & Fogarty, E. A. (2006). Savoring Reading Schoolwide. *Educational Leadership, 64*(2), 32–36.

Reis, S. M., Fogarty, E. A., Eckert, R. D., and Muller, L. M. (2008). *The Schoolwide Enrichment Reading Model reading framework*. Mansfield, CT: Creative Learning Press.

Reis, S. M., Gubbins, E. J., Briggs, C., Schreiber, F. R., Richards, S., Jacobs, J. (2004). "Reading instruction for talented readers: Case studies documenting few opportunities for continuous progress." *Gifted Child Quarterly*, 48, 309–38.

Renzulli, J. S. (1976). The enrichment triad model: A guide for developing defensible programs for the gifted and talented. *Gifted Child Quarterly, 20*(3), 303–306. doi:10.1177/001698627602000327.

Renzulli Center for Creativity, Gifted Education, & Talent Development. (n.d.a). *SEM-R implementation resources.* Accessed April 2, 2018. http://gifted.uconn.edu/semr-resources/.

———. (n.d.b). *SEM-R overview.* Accessed April 2, 2018. http://gifted.uconn.edu/semr-overview/.

———. (n.d.c). *What is the SEM-R?* Accessed April 2, 2018. http://gifted.uconn.edu/semr-about2/Gifted.

Renzulli, J. S. (2011). "What makes giftedness? Reexamining a definition: Giftedness needs to be redefined to include three elements: Above-average intelligence, high levels of task commitment, and high levels of creativity." *Phi Delta Kappan*, 92(8), 81–88. April 2, 2018.

Sohn, E. (2015). Recess: It's important. Does your child get enough of it? *Washington Post*, November 9, 2015. Accessed April 2, 2018. https://www.washingtonpost.com/national/health-science/recess-its-important-does-your-child-get-enough-of-it/2015/11/09/ab610866-8180-11e5-9afb-0c971f713d0c_story.html?utm_term=.ccf51ce6f3f9.

Street, B. (2003). "What's "new" in New Literacy Studies? Critical approaches to literacy in theory and practice." *Current Issues in Comparative Education,* 5(2), 77–91.

Styslinger, M. E., Pollock, T., Lowery, R., and Fink, L. (2010). "The chicken and the egg: Inviting response and talk through Socratic circles." *Voices from the Middle*, 18(2), 36–45.

Tomlinson, C. A., and Eidson, C. C. (2002). *Differentiation in practice: A resource guide for differentiating curriculum, grades K–5.*

Wilson, N., and Bai, H. (2010). "The relationships and impact of teachers' metacognitive knowledge and pedagogical understandings of metacognition." *Metacognition Learning,* 5(3), 269–88.

Wu, E. H. (2013). "The path leading to differentiation: An interview with Carol Tomlinson." *Journal of Advanced Academics*, 24(2), 125–33.

CHILDREN'S BOOKS CITED

Bader, B. (2013). *Who was Christopher Columbus?* New York: Grosset & Dunlap.

Rupert, M. (2008). *Dinosaurs in action: Unearth the secrets behind dinosaur fossils.* New York: Scholastic.

Chapter Five

Nonfiction Instruction for English Language Learners

Xiaodi Zhou and Danling Fu

Schools in the United States have about 10 percent English Language Learners (ELLs), some 4.5 million students, the fastest-growing category of students (NCES, 2015). Among these students, 43 percent begin their US schooling in middle or high school, and 20 percent of high school and 12 percent of middle school ELLs have missed two or more years of school (Fix and Passel, 2003). Preparing these students for their career and college presents a challenge, as they must learn English academic language and content knowledge simultaneously within their limited school time. Therefore, in US language arts classrooms today, a growing trend is the use of nonfiction texts with ELLs as a way to develop their academic language and content knowledge. Nonfiction texts can expand the content repertoire of these students, increasing their English vocabulary in content areas.

NONFICTION INSTRUCTIONAL FRAMEWORK

Using nonfiction has therefore become a key component of language (English or bilingual) and content-integrated education in recent years. Differentiating instruction via such texts can be useful for preparing students of varying degrees of English proficiency and background knowledge. For ELLs, this task can be partitioned into four instructional dimensions (Hernández, 2003):

1. *communication-based instruction*, wherein students learn *in* the target language rather than *about* the language;
2. *content-based instruction*, which involves students not only learning in the target language, but *about* the subject by building meaning from the language;

3. *cognitive development*, which considers instruction that progresses from the concrete to the abstract, and from the figurative to the operational, to facilitate learning for ELLs; and
4. framing *study skills* as learning tools.

This four-dimensional framework structures the delivery of nonfiction material in terms of both form and content, has no sequential orders, and can be used during instruction based on the needs of ELLs. As is evident in Table 5.1, both language and study skill development are aspects of content-based instruction of nonfiction texts. In addition to the content of lessons, the medium and modality are important considerations given the cultural impasse likely experienced by some ELLs. For instance, they may need a quiet space for reading or studying, and/or a means to translate certain English words into their first language. A lack of linguistic development in either the first language or target language can severely hamper their cognitive development.

TEXT SELECTION

It is important to select appropriate texts for instruction. The first decision for teachers to consider in the selection is to choose the best text that supports students' language development concurrent with deepening their content area knowledge. Choosing the most appropriate text can involve many important considerations, such as format, writing style, length, breadth versus depth of material, as well as the students' level of English proficiency and the extent of their background knowledge. Thus, the text should be both challenging and manageable. Failing to choose an appropriate text can cause frustration

Table 5.1.   Instructional Framework Structure at a Glance

Framework Structure	Communication-Based	Content-Based	Cognitive-Based	Study Skills-Based
Feature	English learned through interactions and expressions; direct face-to-face interaction between teacher and student	English, as well as important subject matter knowledge, learned through content instruction	Concrete→ Abstract; Figurative → Operational Careful structuring order of content delivery	Focus, finding a quiet place for concentration, thinking creatively, outside-the-box, etc.

or boredom for the student, as the text can either be too difficult or complex for comprehension, or too simple and uninteresting.

Also, the content can be both culturally familiar and novel, as ELLs can alternate between making personal connections with the text to learning about a new phenomenon. Text selection is then a crucial process that impacts the overall implementation of the course, and structuring the curriculum around certain well-chosen texts can deepen and make the learning more meaningful and authentic for the student.

Content and artwork should also be inviting and interesting to captivate the attention and interest of students. Colorful, vibrant illustrations not only add a concrete visual dimension, but also assist with comprehension by representing the main topics of the text. In this way, ELLs' English proficiencies do not hinder their comprehension, and they can learn from both the visual cues being discussed and the meaning of the English text.

TEXT INCORPORATION

Once an appropriate text has been selected, there are several ways to incorporate the book into the classroom. Texts can be immersed in the curriculum via connecting to ELLs' existing cultural framework or narrative schema. For example, the story of George Washington as the general of the Continental Army and one of the Founding Fathers of the United States may be a familiar story for English native-speaking students, but many ELLs may only superficially know of Washington as the first president of the United States.

Therefore, incorporating a text about Washington, such as Rosalyn Schanzer's (2004) *George vs. George: The American Revolution as Seen from Both Sides*, could also entail some background or contextual information, such as the fact that he had wooden teeth, that he owned slaves, or the anecdote about chopping down the cherry tree. His daring and commendable behavior on the battlefield and as leader of the United States can be balanced with realistic explanations for his victories, such as shifting Britain's military priorities with its conflict with France and its founding of India as its newest colony for the cultivation of tea and tobacco.

This nonfiction text can fit well into a curriculum that seeks to integrate social studies with language arts by supplementing historical or societal content with literary instruction in collaboration between social studies and language arts teachers. ELLs can readily learn important and relevant content that furthers their understanding of the United States and its culture, while supplying a basis for language development with important terms and concepts through cross-curricular integrated learning.

Educators can focus not only on basic comprehension, but also on the deeper meanings (Ferlazzo and Hull-Sypnieski, 2014), for nonfiction can be a platform from which ELLs venture out to higher-level thinking that integrates and compounds multiple layers of knowledge and meanings. Table 5.2 illustrates how students can advance vocabulary from a simple definitional knowledge level (word/idea) to inferring deeper meaning (personal context).

As students talk about and transform data sets from their own first language or any proficient language and heritage culture context, that information is elaborated and synthesized into personalized and bilingual ways of knowing. For example, a Mexican American middle school student, when learning about the American Revolution, can also bring up Hidalgo and the Mexican Revolution against Spain when prompted by the teacher to offer connections to his or her own heritage culture. This student can use Spanish to describe certain terms relating to the event, which personalizes and contextualizes the history, making it more meaningful and authentic.

When guided by the teacher, classmates can also note the similarities and distinctions between the two movements, as the instructor makes a chart of factors on the board to compare the two movements in terms of mother coun-

Table 5.2. Inferring Deeper Meaning from *George vs. George* through Careful Scaffolding

Word/Idea	*Patriots*
Historical Context	Name given to those American colonists who desired independence from Great Britain during the American Revolution in the latter part of the eighteenth century. They fought against the British, established a federal government, and instilled a sense of nationalism in the new country.
Geographical Context	These revolutionaries existed in the thirteen British colonies of North America, spanning the Eastern Seaboard of the continent. Many came from or had roots in Great Britain. There were already distinctions between the desires and priorities of the Northern patriots and the Southern patriots, anticipating the Civil War in the next century.
Personal Context	*Sample Student Response*: As a student, I think of colonists who fought for ideals that they believed in. They were willing to die for these beliefs, in order to gain liberties for themselves and their country. But, another part of me thinks the patriots were just complaining about high taxes and a lack of representation. They espoused ideals of liberty and equality, when those same ideals did not even exist in their own society with Native Americans, African Americans, and women considered second-class citizens.

try, leaders, main causes, results, etc. Other relevant texts for a unit on the American Revolution for middle schoolers can include Elaine Landau's *The Revolutionary War Begins: Would You Join the Fight?* (2010), and Russell Freedman's *Give Me Liberty!* (2002) and *The Boston Tea Party* (2012).

PLANNING FOR INSTRUCTION

Before planning a curriculum for ELLs, instructors need to consider eight key questions (Freeman and Freeman, 2000).

- *Is the curriculum organized around "big" questions?* Instruction is structured around questions that are pertinent to students' lives (e.g., provide a big question and show how it is relevant to a group of students' lives). Bilingual or multilingual nonfiction texts, like *Those Icky Sticky Smelly Cavity-Causing but . . . Invisible Germs* by Judith Anne Rice (2002) and Mao Xiao's (2012) *The Frog and the Boy* can be utilized to connect with students' home languages in Spanish and Chinese, respectively.
- *Are students involved in authentic reading and writing experiences?* Nonfiction texts should deal with issues students care about and are invested in exploring more in depth. Texts such as *Waiting for Wings* (Ehlert, 2001) or *Muhammad* (Demi, 2003) give students opportunities for authentic reading, especially minority students in areas of the country with higher non-majority populations, because they present issues that are pertinent or interesting for many students.
- *Is there an attempt to draw on students' background knowledge and interests, and are they given choices?* Students' funds of knowledge, both linguistic and cultural, can be a rich resource from which to prime learning and integration. Common school standards at times assume students have similar life experiences, so differentiating delivery and assessment is a paramount consideration. Teachers should create spaces and opportunities in their classrooms for students to make connections between their background and new content knowledge, and to choose the language through which students can display their full potential as learners.
- *Is the content meaningful and does it serve a purpose for students?* Language in this context is best learned in the process of studying academic content. Teachers need not devote class periods to defining language but may imply meaning through demonstrations and contextual information. The language becomes real and situated in students' world context. Connecting language to students' lives makes English not just some academic skill they need to master, but a part of their everyday lives and reality.

- *Do students have opportunities to work collaboratively?* Because language acquisition is a social activity, partnering ELLs with native-speaking peers can be beneficial to their cognitive, linguistic, and social development. Teachers may need to decide when to group ELLs with native speakers and when to group ELLs together, because with some tasks, native speakers can assist ELLs with language issues and ELLs can add a fresh perspective unknown to the native speaker. In other tasks, it may be better for students with common language proficiencies or same home language backgrounds to work together, so they are able to develop ideas pertinent to their in-groups (or to use their common home languages).
- *Do students read and write as well as speak and listen during learning?* Students read authentic nonfiction texts of their own choosing—for instance, about the water cycle or regarding the planets in our solar system. Then, they may write in journals and discuss their learning and responses with peers in their choice of language before sharing with the class. They will write individually or as a group and then publish their work regarding learning through these processes. ELLs can also read their own writing, and listen to the works of others, to engage in dialogue with classmates. The input and output of oral and written language of their choice can maximize and greatly enhance ELLs' language and knowledge development.
- *Are students' first language(s) and primary cultures valued, supported, and developed?* Students' first language competencies transfer to their second language, so when their first language is supported and developed, their global language sense is bolstered, and learning the second language is facilitated. Also, reading and learning about their own culture or those of classmates can entail greater appreciation for their own heritage as well as awareness and empathy of others. This type of global awareness nurtures cross-cultural and cross-language encounters.
- *Are students involved in activities that build their self-esteem and provide them with opportunities to succeed?* With this type of instruction, teachers believe and have faith in their students to learn and grasp concepts and content, a process that nurtures self-efficacy. Positive reinforcement and incremental scaffolding of instruction leads students to develop a will to succeed in academics and in their lives. One of the critical considerations when teaching ELLs is scaffolding of instruction, both in terms of depth of material and in terms of language complexity. For example, when asking students to present on a topic related to the American Revolution, instructors can add incremental difficulties in text level to the class each week, asking students to accomplish more in terms of synthesis. Students can first be asked to summarize, then to connect with other movements and with the global social structure, and then finally with themselves to personalize the movement (e.g., How do you relate to the American Revolution today?).

Teachers with ELL students can think about the above issues to best meet the social, linguistic, and cultural needs of these students. Many of these tasks are about bolstering students' self-efficacy while nurturing their appreciation for their own culture and language and those of others and attaining academic achievement.

DEVELOPING ACADEMIC LANGUAGE

Lack of background knowledge and limited English language proficiency may present certain challenges for ELLs in comprehending nonfiction texts. Therefore, teachers need not only to help these students gain background knowledge, but also should create a space for them to make connections between knowledge of their home country and their host country and to value their home language as a learning resource; teachers should systematically guide them to develop their linguistic proficiency to understand nonfiction texts. These strategies will help students better develop their academic language competency. The following are practical suggestions:

- *Activate students' prior knowledge of their home countries (making connections between home and host countries) or let students read about background knowledge in their home language.*

Teachers cannot assume ELLs have the background knowledge required to understand the content featured in nonfiction texts. For example, in reading *George vs. George*, many ELLs may not truly know about the American Revolution, the real lives of the leaders, or the significance of the Declaration of Independence to the American psyche today. To activate these ELLs' prior knowledge, the teacher needs to learn some of the history of the students' home countries and help them make connections with similar historic events in their home countries. Teachers can also let students search online for digital resources in their home language to gain some background knowledge about the American Revolution before reading *George vs. George*.

- *Provide a working bilingual vocabulary list and explain the structure of nonfiction text.*

Nonfiction texts tend to have content-specific academic vocabulary and textual features that are unfamiliar to students. If possible, teachers should provide ELLs with a bilingual key vocabulary list (use a bilingual dictionary or Google Translate) and draw students' attention to the special features of nonfiction texts, such as subtitles, boldface, charts, maps, photos, pictures, and graphs, to help them to better understand the meaning of the text. For those students without strong first language literacy, teachers can utilize visual aids or video materials to help students understand key academic vocabulary and content.

• *Provide students more opportunity to discuss and use academic vocabulary in speaking and writing.*

Since ELLs have little opportunity to hear or use academic vocabulary in their daily lives, teachers should provide class opportunities for them to use academic vocabulary in speaking (group discussion) to each other and writing to present their knowledge. Through speaking and writing with academic vocabulary, ELLs will gain language skills to read nonfiction texts.

• *Help students understand the complex sentence structure in nonfiction texts.*

Nonfiction texts tend to have formal language in complex sentence structures, which may present certain challenges for ELLs' comprehension. Teachers may need to explain linguistic features to students—such as normalization, adverbial and adjective relative clauses, and transitional indications in nonfiction texts—and point out the differences between everyday language and academic language, such as word choice and sentence structure.

SCAFFOLDING INSTRUCTIONAL TECHNIQUES

There are many ways to instruct ELLs with informational nonfiction texts. These tasks help students understand and retain the new material presented in class. One important task is to continually activate or connect with students' background knowledge, whether it be cultural or factual. Teachers also need to continually review and assess students' understanding. There are also strategic components, such as teaching how to take reading notes and engage in rereading, organizing information, predicting, self-questioning, evaluating, monitoring, clarifying, and summarizing. Some popular instructional techniques are illustrated in Table 5.3.

Through these instructional techniques, ELLs can participate in learning the English language while acquiring critical information and knowledge about the world. A specific sample lesson is presented below to demonstrate these instructional techniques.

Applying Instructional Techniques to *George vs. George*

This scaffolded sample lesson plan on the American Revolution is intended for the upper elementary grades or middle school grades (grades 5–8), depending on students' language proficiency level.

Table 5.3.   Some Popular Instructional Techniques

Technique	Activate Prior Knowledge	Instructional Scaffolding	Verbal Scaffolding	Social Component
Description	Teacher can engage in discussion of the broader topic with the class, encouraging peer input and sharing of student experiences and ideas	Use of graphic organizers, partner- and small group-discussion and practice, adapted texts, partially completed outlines, texts with key concepts/ vocabulary highlighted	Guiding students to use language to represent thoughts; verbal scaffolding— think-alouds, paraphrasing, repetition, careful enunciation, review of contextualized vocabulary	Students engage and interact with peers/ instructors; instructors provide opportunities for discussion/ interactions; group work encouraged and nurtured to encourage collaboration and teamwork

1. **Activate Prior Knowledge:** Teachers can introduce this unit with a general discussion of the American Revolution, such as when it happened, why it happened, and some of the consequences. The class can be split up into two groups, the colonists and the British, each coming up with supporting ideas for their side of the struggle. Then, students can discuss important figures in the movement, such as Thomas Jefferson, Benjamin Franklin, Paul Revere, and George Washington. Students can also share what they know about George Washington, such as what state he came from, what was his social status, and what was his role in the American Revolution. Also, students can be given a chance to share ideas about King George III, how long his reign was, and the fact that he established British domination in Europe with the defeat of the French in the Seven Years War and of Napoleon at the Battle of Waterloo, despite losing the American colonies. Teachers can have students brainstorm ideas related to George Washington and King George III, charting their similarities and distinctions in their leadership. Students can compare their backgrounds and the foundations for their respective countries. Also, the topic of national independence can extend to the other national cultures ELLs bring to the classroom, like Mexico, Brazil, or Egypt. ELL's prior knowledge can provide another cultural and historic perspective their mainstream classmates do not share.
2. **Instructional Scaffolding:** Teachers can split students into small groups, with some brainstorming and organizing ideas about Washington and others thinking about King George III. Graphic organizers can record these

ideas, and they can be shared via digital interfaces like Padlet, wherein groups of students can collaboratively input their ideas to be shared digitally with the class in real time. The class can then vote on the most important terms, and they can be recorded and create paragraphs with all the keywords. Finally, partially filled paragraphs with key terms omitted can be written and presented on the overhead or handed out as worksheets. Teachers can also incorporate words in the heritage languages of ELLs to be shared and discussed with the class.

3. **Verbal Scaffolding:** Having already begun the verbal think-alouds in the previous section, there can be more in-depth discussions about each of the key terms. Students can brainstorm terms related to the key terms. There can be repetition of important events, battles, and sites, such as the Declaration of Independence, the Battle of Yorktown, and Mount Vernon. Teachers can also ask ELLs to give the keywords in their heritage languages.

4. **Social Component:** In these groups, students can collaboratively present a facet of either George Washington or King George III's life and share their report with the class. They can perform a skit, reenact an important battle, present a poster, or read a narrative they wrote. One project could be: the students silently act out a scene in one of the Georges' lives and have their classmates guess who and what it is about. Each group member should have a role, and all members should agree upon decisions for the project. Class members should have a chance for a question-and-answer session at the end, and the teacher can ask the final question for each group, which can be answered by anyone in the class. At the conclusion of the presentations, the teacher can also ask the students what they found most interesting about the two Georges. ELL students may give their heritage culture's views of either or both Georges and offer their perception outside of the United States and Great Britain. Also, they can share a central figure in their heritage culture's history, such as Miguel Hidalgo and Mexican independence, and compare him with the colonizing nation's ruler, Ferdinand VII of Spain. Mainstream classmates can react and respond to these connections.

5. **Checking for Understanding and Language Proficiency:** Comprehension of content can be assessed with the question-and-answer session at the end of a presentation, when members go off-script and need to think on their toes. They may need to defend their claims and support their ideas with what they know about either of the Georges and about the contextual historical factors. The teacher can check students' language proficiency, as each student delivers his or her spoken performance and offers verbal feedback of others' performances. Grammar and pronunciation should

be less important than coherence and meaningfulness of message. ELLs can be given specific support based on their demonstrated abilities in the presentations.

ENGLISH LANGUAGE LEARNERS IN THE CLASSROOM

One important consideration for the teacher with ELLs in his or her class-room is to be mindful of the needs of mainstream classmates too. Devoting excess time or individual energy to ELLs on nonfiction texts can alienate mainstream students who may need less time to understand the material. One way to address this issue is to pair ELLs with mainstream students, so that native-speaking classmates can help ELLs learn and understand the text.

Helping ELL students with comprehension and social inclusivity may also help their native classmates increase their own self-esteem and self-efficacy, while deepening their own understanding of the material by teaching or explaining it to others. This task may also help mainstream students gain meta-awareness of the English language.

Instructional techniques may need to be varied to adapt to different contexts with students of different heritage languages or background knowledge. For instance, when discussing the American Revolution, *George vs. George* would be better suited to native speakers in the middle grades given its more difficult language, including terms such as "jubilant" and "unravel." A text like Maestro's (2005) *Liberty or Death: The American Revolution* is also suited to middle grades.

On the other hand, a text like Landau's (2010) *The Revolutionary War Begins* would be better suited to upper elementary students, while Freedman's (2012) *The Boston Tea Party* would be better suited to younger children. Teachers can have a separate lesson plan for ELLs that moves at a slower pace and integrates greater support for language and contextual knowledge.

USING TECHNOLOGY

Another way to assist ELLs' academic learning of nonfiction content is through the use of technology. In today's technology-laden world, many students are highly proficient with technology, including ELLs. Such skills do not necessitate English proficiency, but merely require a familiarity with tech-related devices. With tools such as Google Translate, ELLs can often traverse messy linguistic barriers, or at least minimize them, so their comprehension of the technical language common in many nonfiction texts can improve.

For instance, linguistic barriers students might encounter in *George vs. George* (Schanzer, 2004) include phrases such as "they went to masked balls and the theater, gambled at cards, dice, and roulette, belonged to all sorts of clubs, and met at coffeehouses, taverns, cockfights, chophouses, and pleasure gardens" (p. 13). Unfamiliar terms like "masked balls," "roulette," "taverns," and "chophouses" may hinder understanding of the description of life in England during this time. Using an online dictionary could remedy such problems, and even digital image searches will turn up samples of real-life taverns, for example.

Internet websites and blogs can be useful resources for students whose first language is not English. They can access such sites at their own pace, and search and peruse material at their convenience. One popular and reliable site of interest is www.teachingbooks.net, which offers categories based on grade levels, core curricula, genres, and culture areas, allowing the teacher to match a nonfiction text to a specific student. Nonfiction material is easily accessible these days via the internet, but that material may not always be trustworthy. Such sources can bring a wealth and breadth of data that students may use, but there are also important considerations to temper the unbridled use of online material.

First, critical reading and a healthy skepticism need to foreground any access of internet data. There needs to be a discussion of trustworthy websites versus those that may not be legitimate due to the possibility of frivolous edits. For ELLs, an awareness of being cautious while searching online information is crucial, especially since English may not be their most proficient language. The teacher can have students conduct research on websites with trustworthy data, such as census.gov and Google Scholar, as opposed to Wikipedia or personal blogs.

FINAL THOUGHTS

In this chapter, we have discussed the necessity of using nonfiction texts with ELLs, and the challenges this type of instruction presents. We have discussed how such texts need to be incorporated into the lives of ELLs and that the language elements need not be separately addressed. When language is kept in the context of its usage, such second language elements are situated in their authentic environment, their meaning created in dialogic engagement with the surrounding verbal context. Meaning can more authentically relate to ELL readers and remain with them when they return home. By connecting home literacies with school literacies, ELL students learn the contextual cues that affect and influence language expression in informal and formal settings.

A key consideration in the instruction of ELLs is the notion of language authenticity. Using nonfiction texts can be a great way to bolster ELL students' semantic know-how, while differentiating text complexity can assist with their language acquisition as well. Providing key opportunities for collaboration may assist in their acculturation as well as their sense of in-group identity. Their reading and writing development can be simultaneous, in conjunction with a greater appreciation for their own native languages and cultures.

We believe nonfiction texts can be a great way to reach ELL students in our classrooms. The appropriate nonfiction text, one that suits the semantic and linguistic needs of these students while not alienating mainstream classmates, can benefit all students. Well-designed nonfiction instruction with careful scaffolding will enhance ELLs' academic language and content knowledge development and prepare them for their future. This is a worthy goal.

REFERENCES

Ferlazzo, L., and Hull-Sypnieski, K. (2014). "Teaching argumentative writing to ELLs." *Writing: A Core Skill*, 71, 46–52.

Fix, M., and Passel, J. (2003). U.S. immigration: Trends and implications for school. Paper presented at the National Association for Bilingual Education's "No Child Left Behind" implementation, New Orleans. January 2003.

Freeman, D., and Freeman, Y. (2000). "Meeting the needs of English language learners." *National Council of Teachers of English*, 12, 2–7.

Hernández, A. (2003). "Making content instruction accessible for English Language Learners." In G. C. García (Ed.) *English Learners: Reaching the highest level of English literacy* (125–49). Newark, DE: International Reading Association.

NCES–National Center of Education Statistics. (2015). Accessed April 1, 2018. https:// nces.ed.gov/programs/coe/indicator_cgf.asp.

NONFICTION TEXTS

Demi. (2003). *Muhammad*. New York: Margaret K. McElderry Books.

Ehlert, L. (2001). *Waiting for wings*. Boston, MA: Houghton Mifflin Harcourt.

Freedman, R. (2012). *The Boston Tea Party*. Ill. by P. Malone. New York: Holiday House.

———. (2002). *Give me liberty! The story of the Declaration of Independence*. New York: Holiday House.

Landau, E. (2010). *The Revolutionary War begins: Would you join the fight?* Berkeley Heights, NJ: Enslow Elementary.

Maestro, B. (2005). *Liberty or death: The American Revolution: 1763–1783*. Ill. by G. Maestro. New York: Harper Collins.

Rice, J. A. (2002). *Those icky sticky smelly cavity-causing but . . . invisible germs*. Ill. by J. A. Stricklin. St. Louis, MO: Turtleback.

Schanzer, R. (2004). *George vs. George: The American Revolution as seen from both sides*. Washington, DC: National Geographic.

Xiao, M. (2012). *The frog and the boy*. Ill. by W. Chen. New York: Candied Plums.

Chapter Six

Differentiating and Promoting Critical Thinking with Nonfiction Multimodal Text Sets

Danielle Hartsfield and Nicole Maxwell

Imagine if there was a method that could help you simultaneously address the different personalities, interests, and instructional needs of students in your classroom. And imagine if the processes within that method could also encourage your students to think critically and achieve learning standards in multiple subjects. As we will demonstrate in this chapter, we believe this is possible with multimodal text sets.

Text sets help teachers meet students' various needs and interests while promoting higher-order thinking and addressing English language arts (ELA) and content standards. Text sets can promote critical literacy, too, because they show students multiple perspectives on a topic, event, or issue, particularly perspectives that are sometimes underrepresented in the curriculum. We offer the value of multimodal text sets, the procedures for selecting text set material, and ideas on how text sets enhance literacies. We also describe why and how teachers can utilize them.

Multimodal text sets include print-based items, such as books and magazine articles, as well as electronic resources such as podcasts, websites, and films (Dunkerly-Bean and Bean, 2015). A multimodal text set is a collection of materials focused on a central topic or theme. While fiction and nonfiction pairings are typically included in classroom text sets, our discussion here focuses on multimodal nonfiction text sets.

Quality nonfiction multimodal text sets should include materials appearing in a variety of forms (print-based and electronic), at a range of reading levels, and offering multiple perspectives on the chosen topic or theme (Nichols, 2009). Examples of multimodal text sets appear in the appendix on pages 105–110 and will be referenced throughout. We encourage readers to take a few moments to peruse the examples.

WHY SHOULD TEACHERS USE MULTIMODAL TEXT SETS?

Multimodal text sets are useful for several reasons. For example, they allow teachers to differentiate the way students learn information. Teachers can differentiate by students' interests, learning profiles, and readiness (Tomlinson and Moon, 2013), and multimodal text sets are conducive to each. Although each text set has a central topic, students can explore subtopics according to what piques their individual interests. For example, in a third-grade classroom where students are working with Text Set #1, "Adapting to Survive," a child curious about marine life might select *Glow* (Beck, 2016), which addresses how ocean dwellers use bioluminescence for survival.

Differences in learning profiles are supported when students are given the choice to learn content by reading the books, listening to the podcast, or playing the game included in this text set. Moreover, teachers can account for differences in readiness by including books at various levels of complexity. For instance, proficient readers might appreciate *When Lunch Fights Back* (Johnson, 2015), which has short chapters accompanied by lively photographs, while striving readers will feel confident with *Flying Frogs and Walking Fish* (Jenkins and Page, 2016) or *Creature Features* (Jenkins and Page, 2014), both of which have limited text and supporting images.

Multimodal text sets also invite students to engage in higher-order thinking. To illustrate this point, we use Bloom's revised taxonomy as a framework (Anderson et al., 2001) and Text Set #2, "Creating and Deploying the Atomic Bomb," as an example:

- *Understanding*: Students compare the perspectives in texts. For example, various individuals' reactions to the atomic bomb included in *Bomb* (Sheinkin, 2012) can be compared to those in *Sachiko* (Stelson, 2016), a biography explaining the Nagasaki bombing's tragic impact on a young girl's family.
- *Analyzing*: Students deconstruct the point of view in a nonfiction text. *A Tale of Two Cities*, a video produced by the US War Department (1946), depicts the devastation created by the bombs. Among other possibilities, students might interrogate why the video portrays the destruction of buildings in Hiroshima and Nagasaki and glosses over the impact to humans.
- *Evaluating*: Students critique the points of view presented in the material. For instance, students could judge the persuasiveness of the argument made by former secretary of war Henry Stimson (1947) in "The Decision

to Drop the Atomic Bomb," an article he wrote to justify President Truman's decision.
- *Creating*: Students synthesize ideas from several of the texts to produce something new. Using the resources in this text set, students might create a memorandum convincing President Truman to drop the bomb, or discouraging him from it, and justifying their positions with evidence.

Multimodal text sets with nonfiction materials generally support ELA standards. Students who engage with materials in these text sets and participate in the instructional activities described in this chapter are likely to progress toward proficiency with the College and Career Readiness Anchor Standards (National Governors Association Center for Best Practices & Council of Chief State School Officers, 2010, p. 10).

There are ten College and Career Readiness Anchor Standards for Reading, which serve as the foundation for the Common Core State Standards (CCSS). The anchor standards can be thought of as overarching, broad goals for literacy learning, and they are woven throughout the CCSS for each grade level. Anchor standards 7, 9, and 10 are ones that multimodal text sets are most likely to support:

7. Integrate and evaluate content presented in diverse media and formats, including visually and quantitatively, as well as in words.
9. Analyze how two or more texts address similar themes or topics in order to build knowledge or to compare the approaches the authors take.
10. Read and comprehend complex literary and informational text independently and proficiently.

Additionally, nonfiction materials can support learning in the content areas. To demonstrate this, we have aligned materials in our example text sets to the Next Generation Science Standards ([NGSS]; NGSS Lead States, 2013) and the College, Career, and Civic Life (C3) Framework for Social Studies State Standards (National Council for the Social Studies [NCSS], 2017). Unlike the CCSS for ELA and math, which forty-two states are currently utilizing, there are no nationally adopted science and social studies standards. Instead, individual states usually have their own science and social studies standards.

However, we included the NGSS and C3 Framework because they are current standards written by nationally recognized and respected professional organizations. The NGSS were developed by the National Science Teachers Association, the National Research Council, and the American Association for the Advancement of Science in partnership with twenty-six states that agreed to consider adopting them, while the C3 Framework was designed by the National Council for Social Studies and partner organizations to help states with "upgrading existing social studies standards" (NCSS, 2017, p. 6). Although these standards have not been nationally implemented yet, they may inform the development of states' science and social studies standards in the future; thus, these standards are (or will be) applicable to many teachers and schools. Teachers will also have the opportunity to rethink the standards as applicable to their unique settings.

Furthermore, nonfiction text sets offer students information they may not find in their textbooks. Children's literature, documentaries, and podcasts sometimes feature lesser-known topics, people, and historical events that afford students a richer understanding.

For example, Reese (2008) explains that Native American activism is often excluded from what schools teach about the civil rights movement, and a documentary such as *Alcatraz Is Not an Island* (Ketcheshawno, Plutte, and Fortier, 2001; see Text Set #3) can help make the role of Native Americans more visible. Books like *So You Want to Be President?* (St. George, 2004; see Text Set #4) offer memorable facts that students are unlikely to encounter from both the literacy and social studies curriculum. These nonfiction text sets offer students the opportunity to learn new information and to synthesize ideas across multiple texts and research sources, offering diverse and sometimes unfamiliar viewpoints on a topic.

HOW CAN TEACHERS USE MULTIMODAL TEXT SETS?

There are many ways teachers may use multimodal text sets, including discussions, jigsaws, debates, and research projects. Book discussions are an obvious way of engaging students in text sets; they welcome innovative and student-centered instructional practices that go beyond the traditional literature circle model (Daniels, 2002). These discussions can occur in various formats, such as Socratic Seminar and Think-Pair-Share, among others (see Gonzalez, 2015, for additional ideas).

In each of these formats, students are asked an open-ended question and discuss their thoughts with one student at a time or the whole class. As an example of Think-Pair-Share, the teacher might ask students who have read *We've Got a Job: The 1963 Birmingham Children's March* (Levinson, 2012; see Text Set #3) to consider how social, cultural, and personal factors impacted individual children's decisions to participate in the protests, a question requiring *analysis* (Anderson et al., 2001) of ideas presented in the text. After thinking about this question individually, students would pair up with another student and discuss their ideas, noting similarities and differences. Then, pairs would share their ideas with the whole class.

The Talk Show format (Forest, 2015) is not a new approach to book discussions, but it is an engaging means of helping students consider different viewpoints of an event or issue. In Talk Show, students work in teams to discuss an event or issue presented in a text from the perspective of a certain person. They use evidence from the text to support their ideas about how their assigned person would respond to the event or issue.

After teams have discussed their assigned person's perspective in depth, they elect one team member to sit on a talk show panel. The panel sits in front of the whole class, and students on the panel respond to questions posed by their peers from the perspective of their assigned person. Though students are role-playing while they sit on the talk show panel, they are expected to honor their person's perspective by speaking seriously and respectfully, grounding their responses in facts from the text.

For *We've Got a Job* (Levinson, 2012), students might discuss whether it was justifiable for children to participate in marches and protests. The talk show panel could feature the perspectives of a child marcher, a parent of a child marcher, a teacher whose students left school to participate in the Children's March, and a political or religious leader coordinating the march. In addition to the student panelists, actual participants in civil rights marches could be invited to join the panel virtually via a web conferencing tool like Skype to lend their insight to the conversation. The audience would be encouraged to share their opinions and ask questions, especially of those with lived experiences on the subject. This kind of participation by multiple participants expands the discourse and makes the Talk Show format more innovative.

Talk Show encourages students to consider multiple perspectives of an event or issue presented in a text. The ability to understand texts "from our own perspectives and the viewpoints of others and to consider these various perspectives concurrently" is a foundational skill in developing a critical literacy stance (Lewison, Flint, and Van Sluys, 2002, p. 383). Thus, Talk Show encourages students to view texts through a critical literacy lens.

Another innovative practice that may serve learners well during classroom discussion of texts and expand their research capabilities is Concentric Circles. Also known as the "inside/outside strategy," Jessica Manzone (2015), an instructor of the gifted, notes, "Concentric circles as an instructional strategy provides students with an opportunity to redefine what it means 'to know.'" She adds that "'knowing' something for success in the 21st century, globally competitive society requires a level of analysis that is obtained through multiple examinations of the same subject, topic, or discipline."

It is a useful strategy that encourages learners to be deeply involved in the learning process and demonstrate such commitment by investing a good chunk of their time in researching topics of interest. It also encourages integrated ways of learning, knowing, seeing, and doing that tap on our unique strengths as individuals within a learning community.

Connections become even more important in this era of globalization, and as such, concentric circles "help forge intra-and-inter disciplinary connections by analyzing content from multiple points of view" (Manzone, 2015). Nonfiction texts often provide the basis for transdisciplinary practices that offer a myriad of opportunities for students to explore texts (print, multimodal, and otherwise) by asking a set of questions that allow room for further inquiry. For Manzone (2015), there are some basic questions that can "help students to develop the skills to **circle** the core curriculum with a level of nuanced understanding required of 21st century thinkers." These include:

- Why it is significant, relevant, important, or valuable to the learner?
- When it is important to use it as a scholar of the discipline?
- What are the processes involved in applying it?
- How it is connected to other forms of information?
- What can be modified or adapted to alter its use?
- Who would use the information?
- Where would this information be most appropriate and applicable?

With the Concentric Circles set-up, the circle is important. Students are organized in groups forming inner and outer circles in preparation for an experience with a nonfiction text. They interact with one another, taking turns asking/listening/responding to questions regarding a text. The focus of the discussion is also important as learners engage in discussions that revolve around big ideas, extending the discussion beyond the texts. They make connections between these ideas and society, noting the degree of complexity evident in the information as presented on the topic in comparison to real-life and other sources.

Each student would respond to the classmate situated across from him/her in the opposite circle before rotating to the student next to his/her classmate to listen/respond/pose a question. This rotation would continue until each student has had the opportunity to respond to every student in the opposite circle. In Figure 6.1, we illustrate how students can deepen their understanding of one teenager's contributions to the civil rights movement by participating in a Concentric Circle on *Claudette Colvin: Twice toward Justice* (Hoose, 2009; see Text Set #3).

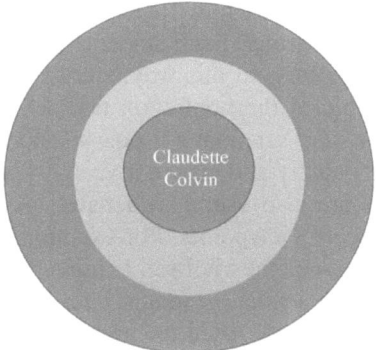

Students discuss questions of increasing complexity, starting with inner circle questions, following with middle circle questions, and ending with outer circle questions.

Inner circle: Students describe facts they know about Claudette Colvin.
- Where was Claudette born and raised?
- What kind of person was Claudette as a child? As a teenager?
- What was Claudette's role in the Montgomery Bus Boycott?

Middle circle: Students elaborate on Claudette Colvin.
- What personal, social, political, and cultural factors led Claudette to act against segregation?
- What are the challenges Claudette faced after she was arrested on the bus?
- Why is Claudette less famous than Rosa Parks even though Claudette was arrested first?

Outer circle: Students make connections to understand Claudette Colvin's role in the bigger picture of the Civil Rights Movement.
- Think about other activists we have read about in this text set. Which activist reminds you the most of Claudette, and for what reasons?
- How were Claudette's goals similar to and different from the goals of civil rights activists from other cultures, such as Mexican Americans and Native Americans?
- What is Claudette's legacy in the Civil Rights Movement?
- If you were asked to make recommendations about what schools should teach about the Civil Rights Movement, would you recommend including Claudette's story in the curriculum? Why or why not? Justify your thinking by synthesizing what you have learned from different sources in the text set.

Figure 6.1. Concentric Circles on *Claudette Colvin: Twice toward Justice* by Phillip Hoose

Using a jigsaw strategy provides the opportunity for students to learn information without having to read, watch, or listen to every text in the text set, making text sets a valuable resource in a time-crunched classroom. In a jigsaw, students break into small groups assigned to research particular items in the text set. They become "experts" on their assigned subtopic and discuss the main points presented in their specific texts. For example, a teacher working with Text Set #5, "Impact of Hurricane Katrina," might assign the subtopic of "impact to animals" to an "expert" group, and students would read *Eight Dolphins of Katrina* (Coleman and Nascimbene, 2013) and *Two Bobbies* (Larson, Nethery, and Cassels, 2008).

Next, "expert" groups disperse into "teaching" groups comprised of one student from each "expert" group. Each student "expert" teaches key points about his/her subtopic to peers. In this way, students piece together the big ideas about the main topic of the nonfiction text set. When coupled with a jigsaw learning strategy, text sets make it possible for students to learn different angles of a topic quickly and efficiently.

Multimodal text sets are also useful in debates because participation requires analysis of divergent viewpoints. For example, a teacher can make a claim such as "The success of the civil rights movement depended on youth activism." The teacher can arrange students into groups and assign them a stance. Then, students can read, listen to, and view materials like those in Text Set #3, "Youth Involvement in Civil Rights," to locate evidence supporting their stance and construct their argument. Students should also be encouraged to find evidence contradicting their stance so they can prepare effective rebuttals. Following this period of researching and building arguments, students could debate their stance in a whole class setting, and ultimately, the class could synthesize the evidence presented to create a class position statement. (See Estes and Mintz's 2016 structured academic controversy model for additional ideas.)

Text sets provide a readily available "library" of references for students to utilize in researching a particular topic for a research project. Students could create numerous products using the information gathered, including digital or print posters, letters to someone of importance to advocate for change, and podcasts.

One example using Text Set #2 would be for a student to assume the role of President Truman in an interview following the drop of the atomic bomb in which his/her classmates act as the interviewers. The interview could be recorded. Along with recording the audio of the interview, students could add applicable images and screenshots of video clips from the text set, crediting the original sources, to accompany the researched information shared in the interview. All of this would then be uploaded as a podcast to be shared with others. A starting point for teachers interested in creating podcasts with their students is ReadWriteThink's (2009) printout, titled "Podcasts: The Nuts and Bolts of Creating Podcasts." Additional resources are also provided on their website.

HOW CAN TEACHERS CREATE MULTIMODAL TEXT SETS?

To begin designing a text set, we suggest teachers utilize the backward design process (Wiggins and McTighe, 2005) by first determining the ELA and/or content standards they want the text set to address. Second, teachers should determine objectives for utilizing the text set to meaningfully support the curriculum. Next, we recommend writing guiding questions for the text set. This ensures the materials eventually selected for the text set are thematically or topically connected, and it narrows down the wide array of materials that could potentially be included. If a potential resource does not help students answer the guiding questions, it should be left out. Once teachers have completed this planning process, it is time to begin searching for materials.

Databases make it simple to locate books on a given topic. We recommend using the Children's Literature Comprehensive Database, which teachers may access through a public or university library. After search terms are entered, results can be filtered by genre, grade, publication date, and award-winning status. Children's book awards can also help teachers locate high-quality materials to include in text sets. Table 6.1 lists well-respected awards honoring nonfiction, though we should note the Notable Social Studies Trade Books for Young People award and *Boston Globe-Horn Book* awards include both fiction and nonfiction.

Magazines should not be overlooked when building text sets. Students enjoy reading them, and the brief, engaging articles are useful for building background knowledge before tackling more difficult texts. Magazines publishing nonfiction articles include *Ask, Dig into History, Muse, Cobblestone, National Geographic Kids, Brainspace, Ranger Rick, Zoobooks*, and the *Kids Discover!* line of magazines. A paid subscription is not always needed to access these magazines; libraries may offer print or online access for free. Some news articles written for children and teens are freely available, including *Smithsonian Tween Tribune* (https://www.tweentribune.com/) and *Time for Kids* (https://www.timeforkids.com/).

Table 6.1. Recommended Book Awards

Award	URL
Boston Globe-Horn Book Awards	http://www.hbook.com/boston-globe-horn-book-awards/#_
Notable Social Studies Trade Books for Young People	https://www.socialstudies.org/publications/notables
Orbis Pictus Award for Outstanding Nonfiction for Children	http://www.ncte.org/awards/orbispictus
Outstanding Science Trade Books for Students K–12	http://www.nsta.org/publications/ostb/
Sibert Informational Book Medal	http://www.ala.org/alsc/awardsgrants/bookmedia/sibertmedal
YALSA Award for Excellence in Nonfiction for Young Adults	http://www.ala.org/yalsa/nonfiction

A well-rounded multimodal text set should include digital materials. Podcasts are useful resources because they can be accessed at any time or place as long as the listener has a phone or computer. Table 6.2 lists several educational podcasts. Though quality documentary films can be located at most public libraries, teachers may also find them on streaming services, such as Netflix (www.netflix.com) and Kanopy (www.kanopystreaming.com).

After compiling possible resources for a text set, teachers should ask the following questions to refine their choices:

- Do the materials align with learning standards and objectives?
- Do the materials address the guiding questions in some way?
- Do the materials address multiple perspectives of the topic?
- Do the materials over- or under-represent certain points of view?
- Do the materials represent a range of reading levels?
- Are the materials accurate and credible?
- Does the text set include materials in different modalities?

Because a text set should be carefully curated, considering these questions is imperative to constructing a quality text set. Once materials have been chosen, teachers may digitally organize their text sets using web tools such

Table 6.2. Educational Podcasts

Name	Description	Website
Brains On!	This podcast addresses science topics and related social problems of interest to children.	https://www.brainson.org /podcast/
But Why	A podcast answering children's questions about the "how" and "why" of natural phenomena, social studies topics, words, and more.	http://digital.vpr.net /programs/why-podcast -curious-kids#stream/0
Revisionist History	Writer Malcolm Gladwell explores unique angles to historical events and current social issues. Best suited for high school and up.	http://revisionisthistory.com/
Stuff You Missed in History Class	Though intended for adults, this podcast about lesser-known historical figures and events can be enjoyed by all.	http://www.missedinhistory .com/
Tumble	Meant for the whole family, this conversational podcast features a variety of science topics.	http://www.sciencepodcast forkids.com/

as Padlet (www.padlet.com) or Pinterest (www.pinterest.com). These tools allow teachers to easily access their text set ideas and add new prospective resources. Teachers can also seek out text sets created by others; several sources are shown in Table 6.3.

FINAL THOUGHTS

Quality multimodal text sets are a versatile method for engaging students in higher-order thinking while working on ELA and content area standards. They allow teachers to differentiate their students' learning based on interests, learning profiles, and readiness since these text sets include print-based and electronic texts at varying levels. These ready-made "libraries" offer a handy resource for involving students in concentric circle discussions, talk show panels, jigsaws, debates, and research projects on particular topics. Through reading, listening, viewing, discussing, and transforming ideas learned from utilizing multimodal

Table 6.3.   Previously Developed Text Sets

Title	Description	Website
Achieve the Core: Text Sets: Building Knowledge and Vocabulary	This website includes professional development on creating text sets, as well as example text sets on various social studies and science topics for K–12 classrooms. The text sets contain names of books, lesson plans, and student handouts.	https://achievethecore.org /category/411/ela-literacy -lessons?filter_cat=1112
Newsela: Featured Text Sets	Text sets for second-grade through twelfth-grade students are featured on the website. Search tools include selecting text sets by reading skill, content provider, and format. Text sets are available in English and Spanish.	https://newsela.com/text-sets/# /featured
Teachers College: The Reading and Writing Project Text Sets	This document includes digital resources for informational text sets created by teachers and shared with Teachers College at Columbia University's Reading and Writing Project.	https://drive.google.com/file /d/0B404rJALRaGwcm JLUXlOYTA1LUU/view

text sets, students gain a deeper, more critical understanding of the topic using interesting and engaging resources. They are also made to see connections between in and- out-of school learning.

In this chapter, we have outlined a rationale for using multimodal text sets and shared text set examples, described in both traditional and innovative ways in which teachers can use them to engage learners, and explained the process for developing text sets. If you have not used text sets in your classroom, we hope you will find the information in this chapter enlightening. Most importantly, we know your students will enjoy the engaging ways of learning information that multimodal text sets can afford.

See the appendix for example text sets.

REFERENCES

Anderson, L. W., Krathwohl, D. R., Airasian, P. W., Cruikshank, K. A., Mayer, R. E., Pintrich, P. R., and Wittrock, M. C. (2001). *A taxonomy for learning, teaching, and assessing: A revision of Bloom's taxonomy of instructional objectives.* New York: Longman.

Beck, W. H. (2016). *Glow: Animals with their own nightlights.* Boston, MA: Houghton Mifflin Harcourt.

Coleman, J. W., & Nascimbene, Y. (2013). *Eight dolphins of Katrina: A true tale of survival.* Boston, MA: Houghton Mifflin Books for Children.

Daniels, H. (2002). *Literature circles: Voice and choice in book clubs and reading groups* (2nd ed.). Portland, ME: Stenhouse Publishers.

Dunkerly-Bean, J., and Bean, T. W. (2015). "Exploring human rights and cosmopolitan critical literacy with global young adult literature multimodal text sets." *NERA Journal,* 50(2), 1–7.

Estes, T. H., and Mintz, S. L. (2016). *Instruction: A models approach* (7th ed.). Boston, MA: Pearson.

Forest, D. E. (2015). "Talk show: A technique to facilitate understanding of story characters." *READ: An Online Journal for Literacy Educators,* 1(1), 53–60. Accessed September 11, 2017. http://digital.library.shsu.edu/cdm/singleitem/collection/p16042coll5/id/1.

Gonzalez, J. (2015). "The big list of class discussion strategies." Cult of Pedagogy; Accessed: August 27, 2017. https://www.cultofpedagogy.com/speaking-listening-techniques/.

Hoose, P. (2009). *Claudette Colvin: Twice toward justice.* New York, NY: Square Fish.

Jenkins, S., & Page, R. (2014). *Creature features: 25 animals explain why they look the way they do.* Boston, MA: Houghton Mifflin Harcourt.

———. (2016). *Flying frogs and walking fish.* Boston, MA: Houghton Mifflin Harcourt.

Johnson, R.L. (2015). *When lunch fights back: Wickedly clever animal defenses.* Minneapolis, MN: Millbrook Press.

Ketcheshawno, M. (Executive Producer), Plutte, J. (Producer), & Fortier, J.M. (Director). (2001). *Alcatraz is not an island* [Motion picture]. United States: Diamond Island Productions.

Larson, K., Nethery, M., & Cassels, J. (2008). *Two Bobbies: A true story of Hurricane Katrina, friendship, and survival.* New York, NY: Walker & Company.

Levinson, C. (2012). *We've got a job: The 1963 Birmingham Children's March.* Atlanta, GA: Peachtree.

Lewison, M., Flint, A. S., and Van Sluys, K. (2002). "Taking on critical literacy: The journey of newcomers and novices." *Language Arts*, 79(5), 382–92.

Manzone, J. (2015). Concentric Circles: A curricula approach. Accessed October 5, 2017. http://giftededucationcommunicator.com/gec-spring-2015/concentric-circles -a-curricular-approach/.

National Council for the Social Studies. (2017). *The College, Career, and Civic Life (C3) Framework for social studies state standards: Guidance for enhancing the rigor of K–12 civics, economics, geography, and history.* Silver Spring, MD: NCSS. Accessed August 23, 2017. https://www.socialstudies.org/sites/default/files/2017 /Jun/c3-framework-for-social-studies-rev0617.pdf.

National Governors Association Center for Best Practices & Council of Chief State School Officers. (2010). *Common core state standards for English language arts and literacy in history/social studies, science, and technical subjects.* Washington, DC: Author. Accessed August 23, 2017. http://www.corestan dards.org/ela-literacy.

Next Generation Science Standards Lead States. (2013). *Next Generation Science Standards: For states, by states.* Washington, DC: The National Academies Press. Accessed August 23, 2017. https://www.nextgenscience.org/sites/default/files/NGSS %20DCI%20Combined%2011.6.13.pdf.

Nichols, M. (2009). *Expanding comprehension with multigenre text sets.* New York: Scholastic.

ReadWriteThink. (2009). "Podcasts: The nuts and bolts of creating podcasts." Podcast accessed August 25, 2017. http://www.readwritethink.org/files/resources/printouts /Podcasts.pdf.

Reese, D. (2008). "Subjects not taught: American Indian activism, and, code talkers." American Indians in Children's Literature; February 3. https://americanindians inchildrensliterature.blogspot.com/2008/02/subjects-not-taught-american-indian .html.

Sheinkin, S. (2012). *Bomb: The race to build and steal-the world's most dangerous weapon.* New York, NY: Roaring Brook Press.

St. George, J. (2004). *So you want to be president?* Ill. Small, D. New York, NY: Philomel Books.

Stelston, C. (2016). *Sachiko: A Nagasaki bomb survivor's story.* Minneapolis, MN: Carolhoda.

Stimson, H. L (1947). *The decision to use the atomic bomb.* http://afe.easia.columbia. edu/ps/japan/stimson_harpers.pdf. Accessed August 18, 2017.

Tomlinson, C. A., and Moon, T. R. (2013). *Assessment and student success in a differentiated classroom.* Alexandria, VA: ASCD.

U.S. War Department. (1946). *A tale of two cities* [video file]. Accessed August 18, 2017. https://archive.org/details/TaleofTw1946.

Wiggins, G., and McTighe, J. (2005). *Understanding by design* (2nd ed.). Alexandria, VA: ASCD.

Chapter Seven

Creating an Appealing and Usable Classroom Library of High-Quality Diverse Nonfiction Texts

Cuthbert Rowland-Storm

A fourth-grade boy wanders into his classroom library to book shop. He is of Japanese, Vietnamese, Mexican, and Native American descent. He loves video games and science. He glances at the same books he always sees, with adults and children with white skin engaging in exciting science explorations, but decides they are not for him. He chooses the same book about frightening and poisonous animals that he has already borrowed five times.

The dilemma he faces—that of a very white nonfiction section in his classroom library—is quite common, and teachers often find it difficult to fix. Whether a classroom reflects the United States' ethnic and cultural diversity, or only represents one or two ethnic or cultural groups, students deserve and require a classroom library that is not culturally monotone—or monotonous.

Even in a classroom that appears to have students of very similar ethnicity, class, ability, and cultural values, there will be a diversity of interests within the classroom. Because a classroom library is a place for learning, the ability to branch out from one's immediate interests should also be fostered and encouraged.

It is also often difficult to find diverse nonfiction in public school libraries. For research on this chapter, the author spoke with school librarian Christopher Robert, who was a classroom teacher for twenty years in Title I and ethnically diverse or majority minority schools in Los Angeles and Seattle, before becoming a school librarian. He is disappointed in the lack of quality diverse nonfiction that he has access to for his library. With his deep commitment to honoring his students' experiences, he says there just isn't enough diverse nonfiction children's books out there.

Even when a teacher holds Rudine Sims Bishop's (1990) conviction that books can and should be mirrors, windows, and sliding glass doors, sometimes just finding those books can seem very difficult. Once those books and other texts are found, presenting them in a way in which students will access them remains another distinct challenge. It is easy to rely on simply dividing the books between fiction and nonfiction, sometimes pulling out biographies or animal books, as many classroom libraries do, but a teacher who truly wants students to find quality, diverse nonfiction texts has to do some careful curating and organizing to truly get them into students' hands.

This chapter shares some ideas on how to organize a classroom library in order to make high-quality nonfiction texts—texts that respectfully include people who are underrepresented—prominent and easily accessible to readers. If the library has diverse nonfiction texts that are not used, this may teach students in the classroom that those topics are less important than those that are in high circulation.

MAKING YOUR NONFICTION LIBRARY APPEALING

Readers come to nonfiction in different ways: for pleasure, as browsers, and as learners. If a teacher feels tied to a level system, there is freedom in nonfiction, as students are able to enjoy and learn from images, captions, graphs and charts, and section headings. At the same time, due to academic language, some nonfiction can be and feel inaccessible to less-practiced readers.

Teachers can read these books along with students, suggest a stronger reader with similar interests as a buddy, and provide supplemental materials to help scaffold readers' understanding of difficult words and concepts. A teacher may need to help students understand how to select nonfiction books of interest, how to use nonfiction books, or how to understand why a particular topic is interesting.

Student Interests

When students "engage in activities they feel are important," they can "do work that historians, anthropologists, or physical scientists perform" (Kincheloe and Steinberg, 1998, p. 15). Attitude and interest surveys can provide information about topics that students want to read about. Start with the interests of the most reluctant readers, even interviewing them for deeper insight (Worthy, 1996, p. 491).

Connecting with families and community members to learn about topics that are important to students and their communities is also a way to help enrich the library in a way that appeals to students. While the appeal of having parents come in to promote topics or books varies by age, community members could also come in and talk up books or topics that could be found in the classroom library.

In his school library, Christopher Robert stocks and promotes graphic novel format texts about civil rights leaders and black heroes of the revolutionary war. Sports books are perennial favorites, but although he intentionally carries a number of sports books about women, they rarely get checked out. This may be because boys "are more apt than girls to closely guard the gendered boundaries of their reading (in public)" (Dutro, 2001, p. 383). As a classroom teacher, you can engage in educational activities that counter those ideas or at least get students looking at those books.

One thing to keep in mind is something we know as readers but sometimes forget as teachers: there are many facets to what makes a book appealing. Young readers who may only be able to find a book or two that reflects specific interests or experiences may have a hard time articulating why a certain book may or may not be right for them, but it is a good idea to respect their opinions.

This can be frustrating for a teacher who puts a lot of effort into their library, but it's important not to take it personally. It may be difficult to examine and purchase new books each year, which is part of why utilizing school and local libraries can be so helpful.

Student Needs

Along with student choices are student needs. Meeting the needs of disabled students and students who are developing their English or reading skills can improve their access to information and provide them with independence (Hopkins, 2004, p. 16). Books with different print and font sizes support many readers.

Some students may need texts in multiple languages, including picture dictionaries (Neuman, 2001, p. 13). These books can be hard to come by, but students are more likely to read them if the books' languages are marked in some clearly visible way. The National Center on Cultural and Linguistic Responsiveness's guide on Selecting Culturally Appropriate Children's Books in Languages Other Than English (https://eclkc.ohs.acf.hhs.gov/hslc/tta-system/cultural-linguistic/fcp/docs/ncclr-qguide-select-cultural-childrens-books-non-english.pdf) is full of resources for finding, evaluating, and using books in other languages.

It is also beneficial to English language learners and other readers to have books with labeled pictures (Neuman, 2001, p. 13). Even unlabeled picture books can help visually provide cues that can help English language learners understand unfamiliar English vocabulary (Agosto, 2007, p. 28). Color coding or other clear visual supports can help students find books that interest them.

Visual Supports and Realia

Posters and realia can make the topics in a classroom library become more understandable and draw readers in. They can make the space and its texts more inviting. At the same time, as Naidoo and Crandall (2010) point out regarding objects related to Latino and indigenous culture, it is important to make sure the objects are more than just decorations and their "authentic and symbolic uses" are honored. They also suggest inviting "artists and family members" to "share the significance of various items" (p. 121).

Lots of Choices

Try to have picture books and denser, more text-heavy books on the same or complementary topics. Students can use the simpler texts to build vocabulary and content knowledge that will help them access the more difficult texts. It can let the same student explore the same topic in different ways, or can promote study of a topic of interest among friends.

Picture books are beneficial for elementary and secondary classrooms because the illustrations can make the learning more real, and they are also likely to reflect the social history of people and their lives, which can counter dominant and Eurocentric perspectives (O'Brian and Cruz, 2014, p. 67).

Christopher Robert has noticed that shiny new books get a lot of attention, and highlighting them is useful. However, he notes that variety in and of itself is attractive for young readers. He uses the heritage months to intentionally buy and showcase books about underrepresented groups.

While it's tempting to think of a diverse nonfiction library as a goal to achieve, Crisp et al. (2016) remind us that "we cannot acquire a set of books and then check 'diverse classroom/school library' off our to-do lists," because "cultural issues, relationships, languages, and understandings shift and change across time and context, and we need to be evaluating the contents of our libraries on an ongoing basis" (p. 39).

ARRANGING THE BOOKS WITHIN THE SPACE

Christopher Robert observed a positive change in how students accessed his library and its topics once he added illustrated foam core shelf placards to highlight topics in his collection. Make your students aware of your organizational system and clearly label your collection.

Student Voice in Organization

Jones (2006) suggests involving students in the process of library organization. This allows students to understand the organization of their own classroom library, and they often get excited about discovering the books in the library, distracting themselves from organizing by reading them (which may be the teacher's goal after all). She also suggests creating a color code and an easily accessible key. Students' perspectives can give fresh eyes to how diverse a library is, as well as places where there can be more representation (Crawling out of the Classroom, 2016).

Text Connections

To amplify a nonfiction collection, group sets of texts around a theme. A text set can encourage intertextual links and connections, as nonfiction and fiction texts can provide background knowledge for each other. Make sure your text sets "represent a variety of genres and are on varying readability levels" (Smolen and Oswald, 2010, p. 23).

Another way to connect texts is to make curricular connections between social studies and science. Agosto (2007) points out that integrating multicultural resources with each other teaches students that there are variant perspectives on most issues, and cultural background plays a large part in one's interpretation (p. 28). Naidoo (2010c) provides a good example of a class-wide research project that uses a novel read-aloud, class discussion, student access to web resources, fiction books, and nonfiction books to create a website sharing opposing viewpoints about immigration and deportation (pp. 301–2).

Reading Level

A classroom library needs a wide variety, spanning a wide range of difficulty levels (Neuman, 2001, p. 12). What matters may not be steering a student to the right book level, but instead having multiple book levels available, especially with nonfiction, where students can build content vocabulary from simpler texts and use the illustrations of complex texts to enhance comprehension.

Rotating Collection

Neuman (2001) recommends having both a core/permanent collection and a revolving collection, based on curriculum or current student interests (p. 13).

As a teacher, Christopher Robert would check out two hundred books at a time from his school library to supplement his permanent collection. As a school librarian, he is very happy to pull books for teachers. He says it's his job and not only does he enjoy it, but it proves to himself and the school district that his job, is important. Many schools in the United States no longer have libraries or librarians, but public librarians are always happy to help. Letting librarians know about diverse books and requesting them promotes those books.

An Attractive Setting

Neuman (2001) suggests partitions, space for four or five students, comfortable furniture, plants, a variety of types of book displays, and props (p. 13), and Fractor, Woodruff, Martinez, and Teale (1993) recommend at least eight books per child and naming the space (p. 479) (which could be in English or in another language that represents your students [p. 482]). The level of privacy that is appropriate or needed, the absorbency of the furnishings, and the types of displays and props, which may vary by age of the students, are all useful to consider.

It is important to also make space for the ideas that the nonfiction collection brings up. This can be research on one's own life or the local area. It can also be space made within the day for conversations about books, or spaces within the actual library for conversations. There could be a paper graffiti wall for thoughts on books, recommendation cards, or a blank book for recording thoughts. Among the other visuals in the classroom library, the readers in the classroom could find prompts for conversation—questions and/ or sentence stems to get the conversation flowing (see Table 7.1).

It can be hard to give up the idea that reading must always be a silent, solitary experience, but that doesn't work for all readers, and nonfiction provides a perfect opportunity for conversation. Worthy (1996) shares wisdom from a librarian who says, "Students want to read more when their teachers think of free reading as a time of enjoyment rather than an assignment" (p. 490).

Table 7.1. Example Questions Suggested by Pinnell and Fountas (2007)

What do you already know about this topic?
What connections can you make to other books?
Have you changed your mind after reading this book?
How well do you think the author used illustrations and graphics? How did they help you as a reader?
What else would you have included if you were the author?
What did the author do that made this book interesting?
What qualifications does the author have to write an informational text?
How does this book give you a new perspective?
Are the social issues/cultural groups in the text accurate? Why or why not?

CURATING YOUR LIBRARY

To engage students as readers, teachers need a lot of books. Although books that are produced by textbook companies for an educational market may be easier to come by, authentic texts are more likely to engage readers into becoming lifelong readers. Crisp et al. (2016) provide questions to ask when considering the diversity of one's classroom library. These include: "What is included in my classroom library when I think about depictions of gender? How does my library look when I think about racial diversity? Who has voice and representation here? Who does not?" (p. 39).

CONSIDERATIONS

Curricular

A teacher must consider both what their students are interested in and how the books that they are choosing can complement the lessons they will be formally teaching. If the teacher intentionally ties their library into the curriculum and builds a personal familiarity with those texts, they can make suggestions based on what their students are showing interest in and have richer conversations (Grant, 2004, p. 35).

Underrepresented Topics

While it may feel and be risky to include texts in a classroom library about controversial topics such as race relations, gender equality, sexuality, gender identity, globalization, immigration, refugees, terrorism, fair trade, climate change, and social media, the inclusion of texts about sensitive topics can increase student engagement. Popular culture can be a catalyst for exploring sensitive and controversial topics too. Students' connection to popular culture can be "linked to their memberships in families and neighborhoods and to the forms of pleasure, power, and companionship they found there" (Dyson, 2003, p. 329), and can bring about stronger engagement with the nonfiction topics they associate with popular culture.

Authorship/Authenticity

A concern for a classroom teacher is that of authorship and authenticity (see Fox et al. [2003], for an extended discussion of this complex issue). Many published authors are white, even when the topic is people of color, and books about people with disabilities are rarely written by people with those disabilities. Thus, books need to be examined carefully, especially older books. As Naidoo (2010a) highlights, old books about Latinos in the United States were nearly always written by "non-Latinos who had visited these countries a few times and wanted to highlight the 'costumes' of the people and their unusual customs" (p. 50). Difficult titles can be used instructionally, encouraging students to think about important textual elements such as perspective. Nonfiction is necessarily a product of its time and its authors, and this skepticism is useful for approaching any text that claims to be true.

Cultures and groups of people are diverse. Even though both cultures are Latino, a book about a Mexican scientist may not resonate with a student from Cuba, because each Latino culture is unique (Naidoo, 2010b). It also may not resonate with a student from Mexico because each person is unique, including within cultural groups.

Also, even though you may cultivate your library with students' individual cultures and experiences in mind, there are few instances where it is appropriate to base a recommendation to a student solely on a cultural or family similarity. Students with same-sex parents may steer clear of books about that topic, due to over-familiarity and unease about standing out. Curt Dudley-Marling's (1997) experience as a classroom teacher led him to the conclusion that "to the degree that my use of multicultural literature marked some of my students as *different*, I may have undermined these students' own efforts to become mainstream Canadian" (p. 159).

Media Other Than Books

Magazines can complement and support the rest of your nonfiction library. They often present information in a short, appealing way. There are children's magazines available in other languages as well, and while a subscription may be fairly expensive, it may be less expensive than four or six or twelve educational titles in a foreign language (see Naidoo and Crandall, 2010, for suggestions of Spanish and bilingual magazines).

Audio versions of texts (which could be professionally produced by the publisher of the book, available to listen to online, or produced by the teacher, students, families, or community members) can scaffold understanding of texts for students who find a certain text challenging or who are English language learners, helping students build vocabulary and academic schema (Zimmerman, Rasinski, and Foreman, 2010, p. 379). They are also useful for students with visual impairments or who have other disabilities that affect their ability to access print (Hopkins, 2004, p. 16). Audiovisual materials, such as documentaries and some web content, can help students understand the multiple perspectives in social studies, science, and other fields (Burrows and Keiner, 2014, p. 156).

Web sources can provide more current information than books can (Naidoo and Crandall, 2010, p. 114) and English language learners may find the visual supports of short web pages useful (Agosto, 2007, p. 28).

Teacher- and Student-Created Texts

If a teacher wants to provide texts that interest their students, and those texts are not immediately available, the teacher can create texts for the classroom library or encourage students to create texts that can become part of the classroom library for future students. Student-created texts introduce new students to the importance of reading, writing, and their own voice within the classroom (Brassell, 1999, p. 651).

TEXT SOURCES

Book Lists

Often, when looking for diverse nonfiction books, a teacher has to find either lists of nonfiction books and look for diversity or find lists of diverse and multicultural books and look for nonfiction. It may be more useful to do the latter, combing lists about diverse populations for nonfiction titles because the likelihood that the list maker is culturally sensitive is higher. However, this often requires you to read individual book descriptions to decipher if a book is nonfiction before you can start to think if the particular title is appropriate for your collection.

The We Need Diverse Books project has been powerful, and their website has a strong list of links (http://weneeddiversebooks.org/where-to-find-diverse-books/) to collections of diverse books, but it does not focus on nonfiction. The website also includes links to other lists that include nonfiction texts, although discovering which lists contain nonfiction books takes some careful discernment. Teaching for Change, Latinxs in Kid Lit, and the Anti-Defamation League are other sources for diverse nonfiction texts. Parenting blogs, such as Mom.me, also serve as important resources, but teachers need to be mindful of the fact that these books are not necessarily recommended by educators.

Awards

Besides searching through these lists, books that have won awards are a good starting point. As librarian Christopher Robert points out, these have already been vetted, which reduces some of the anxiety around appropriateness and authenticity. Nonetheless, just because a book has won an award does not mean it is not flawed or incomplete. Some awards are specific to a cultural group but may not necessarily focus on nonfiction, so one has to sort through titles carefully (see Table 7.2).

It can seem intimidating, but a nonfiction collection draws and supports readers looking for mirrors, windows, and sliding glass doors when teachers draw

Table 7.2. Awards

Award Focus	Award Title	Award Association or Organization	Children's Book Award Established
Africa	Children's Africana Book Awards (CABA)	Africa Access and the Outreach Council of the African Studies Association	1992
African American	Coretta Scott King Award	American Library Association	1970
African American	NAACP Image Awards	National Association for the Advancement of Colored People	1996
American Indian/Native American	American Indian Youth Literature Award	American Indian Library Association	2006
Asian Pacific American	Asian/Pacific American Award for Literature	Asian Pacific American Library Association	2001
Disability	Schneider Family Book Award	American Library Association	2004
Disability	Dolly Gray Award	Council for Exceptional Children	2000
Jewish	Sidney Taylor Book Award	Jewish Libraries	1968
Latino	Pura Belpré Award	American Library Association	1996
LGBT	Lambda Literary Awards	Lambda Literary Foundation	1994
LGBT	Stonewall Book Awards	American Library Association	2010
Mexican American	Tomás Rivera Book Award	Texas State University	1995
South Asia	South Asia Book Award	South Asia National Outreach Consortium	2012
Multicultural	Notable Books for a Global Society	Children's Literature and Reading Special Interest Group of the International Literacy Association	1996
Multicultural	Skipping Stones Honor Award	Skipping Stones	1988
Feminist	Amelia Bloomer Book List	American Library Association	2002
Peace and Social Justice	Jane Addams Children's Book Award	Jane Addams Peace Association	1953
Tolerance, Diversity, and Social Justice	Once Upon a World Children's Book Award	Museum of Tolerance	1996 (final award was 2014)

Award Focus	Award Title	Award Association or Organization	Children's Book Award Established
Nonfiction	Orbis Pictus Award for Outstanding Nonfiction	National Council of Teachers of English	1989
Nonfiction	Next Generation Indie Award for Children's/ Juvenile Nonfiction	Independent Book Publishing Professionals Group, Allen O'Shea Literary Agency	2007
Nonfiction	Young Adult Library Services Association's Award for Excellence in Nonfiction	American Library Association	2010
Nonfiction	Robert F. Sibert Informational Book Medal	American Library Association	2001
Nonfiction	Boston Globe-Horn Book Award (Nonfiction Category)	Boston Globe-Horn Book	1967
Nonfiction	International Literacy Association Children's and Young Adults' Book Awards (Nonfiction Category)	International Literacy Association	1975
Nonfiction and Fiction	Notable Children's Books	American Library Association	1940
Ethnically-Focused Social Studies Text	Carter G. Woodson Book Award	National Council for the Social Studies	1974

from the many resources available to them to find, organize, promote, and teach diverse nonfiction texts. Hopefully this chapter can make those resources seem closer and easier to use than they were before, and will empower teachers and school librarians to make informed, confident decisions about their diverse non-fiction library in the best interest of their students.

REFERENCES

Agosto, D. E. (2007). "Building a multicultural school library: Issues and chal-lenges." *Teacher Librarian*, 34(3), 27–31.

Bishop, R. S. (1990). "Mirrors, windows, and sliding glass doors." *Perspectives*, 6(3), ix–xi.

Brassell, D. (1999). "Creating a culturally sensitive classroom library." *The Reading Teacher,* 52(6), 651–52.

Burrows, A., and Keiner, J. (2014). "The social side of science." In T. Lintner (Ed.), *Integrative strategies for the K–12 social studies classroom* (149–65). Charlotte, NC: Information Age.

Crawling out of the Classroom. (May 7, 2016). "Having students analyze our classroom library to see how diverse it is." Accessed April 30, 2017. https:// crawlingoutoftheclassroom.wordpress.com/2016/05/07/having-students-analyze -our-classroom-library-to-see-how-diverse-it-is/.

Crisp, T., Knezek, S. M., Quinn, M., Bingham, G. E., Girardeau, K., and Starks, F. (2016). "What's on our bookshelves? The diversity of children's literature in early childhood classroom libraries." *Journal of Children's Literature*, 42(2), 29–42.

Dudley-Marling, C. (1997). *Living with uncertainty: The messy reality of classroom practice.* Portsmouth, NH: Heinemann.

Dutro, E. (2001). "'But that's a girls' book!' Exploring gender boundaries in children's reading practices." *The Reading Teacher*, 55(4), 376–84.

Dyson, A. H. (2003). "'Welcome to the jam': Popular culture, school literacy, and the making of Childhoods." *Harvard Educational Review*, 73(3), 328–61.

Fox, D. L., Short, K. G., and National Council of Teachers of English, Urbana, IL. (2003). *Stories matter: The complexity of cultural authenticity in children's literature.* Urbana, IL: National Council of Teachers of English.

Fractor, J. S., Woodruff, M. C., Martinez, M. G., and Teale, W. H. (1993). "Let's not miss opportunities to promote voluntary reading: Classroom libraries in the elementary school." *The Reading Teacher*, 46(6), pp. 476–84.

Grant, R. (2004). "Science libraries in the classroom." *Green Teacher*, 74, 35–38.

Hopkins, J. (2004). "School library accessibility: The role of Assistive Technology." *Teacher Librarian*, 31(3), 15–18.

Jones, J. A. (2006). "Student-involved classroom libraries." *The Reading Teacher*, 59(6), 576–80.

Kincheloe, J. L., and Steinberg, S. R. (1998). "Making meaning and analyzing experience—student researchers as transformative agents." In J. Kincheloe and S. Steinberg (Ed.), *Teachers' Library: Students as Researchers: Creating Classrooms that Matter.* Bristol, PA: Falmer Press, pp. 228–242.

Naidoo, J. C. (2010a). "A brief historical overview of Latino children's literature in the United States." In J. C. Naidoo (Ed.), *Celebrating cuentos: Promoting Latino children's literature and literacy in classrooms and libraries* (45–57). Santa Barbara, CA: Libraries Unlimited.

———. (2010b). "Developing and enriching comunidad: Reaching out to Latino communities via public and school libraries." In J. C. Naidoo (Ed.), *Celebrating cuentos: Promoting Latino children's literature and literacy in classrooms and Libraries* (239–57). Santa Barbara, CA: Libraries Unlimited.

———. (2010c). "Using print and digital Latino children's books to promote multiple literacies in classrooms and libraries." In J. C. Naidoo (Ed.), *Celebrating cuentos: Promoting Latino children's literature and literacy in classrooms and libraries* (301–17). Santa Barbara, CA: Libraries Unlimited.

Naidoo, J. C., and Crandall, H. (2010). "Latino children's literature and literacy in school library media centers." In J. C. Naidoo (Ed.), *Celebrating cuentos: Promoting Latino children's literature and literacy in classrooms and libraries* (113–43). Santa Barbara, CA: Libraries Unlimited.

Neuman, S. B. (2001). "The importance of the classroom library." *Early Childhood Today*, 15(5), 12–14.

O'Brian, J., and Cruz, B. C. (2014). "Making social studies accessible and engaging for English Language Learners." In T. Lintner (Ed.), *Integrative strategies for the K–12 social studies classroom* (63–82). Charlotte, NC: Information Age.

Smolen, L. A., and Oswald, R. A. (2010). *Multicultural literature and response: Affirming diverse voices*. Santa Barbara, CA: Libraries Unlimited.

Worthy, J. (1996). "Removing barriers to voluntary reading for reluctant readers: The role of school and classroom libraries." *Language Arts*, 73(7), 483–92.

Zimmerman, B., Rasinski, T., and Foreman, T. (2010). "Reading fluency and multicultural literature." In L. A. Smolen and R. A. Oswald (Ed.), *Multicultural literature and response: Affirming diverse voices* (371–402). Santa Barbara, CA: Libraries Unlimited.

Conclusion

A Few Thoughts on Using Nonfiction Texts in the Twenty-First-Century Classroom

Paul H. Ricks

It's somewhat tempting to look at the myriad changes and improvements that have been made in contemporary nonfiction texts for young readers and feel like most of the job has already been done for us. After all, with nonfiction texts that now look more like comics, with many innovatively expanding our definitions of what we understand to be nonfiction literature, and with visionary authors and illustrators who breathe new life into nonfiction by reimagining the ways "true" stories can be told, it might seem as if there's no way to go wrong. All we really need to do is match inquisitive Student X with well-crafted Book Y and wait for the revolution, right? Most educators will agree that it's rarely that easy. A good text in the right hands can work wonders, but if that's all it really takes to promote student engagement and learning, I daresay we would have figured it all out by now.

* * *

My five-year-old son and some of my students in their early twenties recently asked very similar questions based on what they had been reading. My son was reading a book about various Tyrannosaurs, and when he saw an illustration depicting one that was as long as a bus he asked, "Dad, is that real? How do we know that T-Rex was really as big as a bus?" We then looked up some information online showing the fossils found at various dig sites, with various 3D renderings of what they might have looked like when they were alive, and it was fascinating for both of us to learn and remember that Tyrannosaurs weren't even the largest dinosaurs out there.

That same day, my students, who are all preservice teachers, met in literature groups to discuss various biographies and informational texts they had read for class. During one conversation, a student turned and asked, "Mr. Ricks, how do we know all this is even real? I mean, can't anyone just make something up, say a story is true, and then get away with whatever they want?" Many of my other students had similar questions, as they were slow to accept that authors hadn't taken significant liberties to make their stories more exciting and enticing. We discussed how good nonfiction authors will include notes and references to substantiate their claims and descriptions, but even so, it took a while for some of my students to believe that all the information presented in the various texts was "true."

It has been my experience that twenty-first-century students are quite skeptical—as they have every reason to be—and I imagine that they will only become more so moving forward. With highly staged "reality" television, with various media outlets "telling it like it is" but agreeing on essentially nothing, with films "based on true stories" that often employ fabricated characters and fictionalized plotlines, and with such overwhelming amounts of contradictory information made all the more accessible in this technological age, it makes sense to me that our students will not be overly accepting of everything given them, nonfiction texts included.

Rather than thinking of our students as world-weary and cynical, however, I wonder if we might reframe their collective skepticism as a possible source of strength rather than weakness. Such skepticism will potentially keep them safe from various harms (e.g., credit card scams, virus-laden emails, cyber relationships based on false identities), and their willingness to question the reliability of a source may well prove to be an important way to survive in a world where the lines that separate fact from fiction are increasingly blurred.

Additionally, their skepticism can serve as an incentive for educators who need to attain more expertise, as we all do. We, too, should be asking, "How can we even know if this is real?" If our lessons about the discovery of electricity, the ceremonial rituals in ancient Egypt, the larger-than-life historical figures, or the planet-saving wonders of recycling seem overly idyllic, then perhaps what we're teaching should be reconsidered. Our students are going to question everything, and I like to think that we and they will be better for it.

* * *

Educators and students are currently surrounded by never-before-seen quantities of information. The frenetic pace with which this information is shared can make us feel like our reflexes and reactions must be as fast as the information presented to us. We impulsively "like" or "dislike" in an effort to keep up, with our opinions being shouted from the rooftops before we've even reached the end of the video clip or soundbite. We also often disregard huge chunks of information altogether because we feel paralyzed by the abundance that is beyond our ability to comprehend in the moment. Many of our students cannot remember a time when such was not the norm.

For those of us who love books and want to share our enthusiasm for them with our students, we might wonder if printed texts can compete with the various electronic devices that are so prevalent today. It's not that we think reading will somehow disappear entirely, but because we can't predict the future with any type of certainty, we question whether we are adequately prepared for it. Are printed texts outmoded? Will book clubs and discussion groups be predominantly comprised of luddite educators nostalgically trapped in the not-so-distant past? Is it even worthwhile to think of the ways we can incorporate nonfiction texts into our instruction when it seems like we might be moving in directions that could essentially render them obsolete?

I don't think so. I don't pretend to have all, or even most, of the answers educators might be looking for—though the authors of the preceding chapters have given some rather wonderful insights and ideas that I'm excited to try. I do believe, however, that as we attempt to enhance young readers' understandings of the world through their experiences with nonfiction texts, we will find ourselves pleasantly surprised by their relevance to our students' lives. For all our technological developments, even the most advanced machines have yet to satisfy all our curiosities. And for all our impatient rushing to make sense of the world, we have yet to find anything quite like a good book that allows us to slow down and thoughtfully contemplate what it all might mean.

The purpose of this book is to support educators and students who wish to critically and creatively engage with nonfiction texts. Some of the heavy lifting has been done for us, with authors and illustrators crafting exceptional works that beg to be pondered and appreciated, evaluated and interrogated. But to really make any headway with our twenty-first-century students, we need to recognize that their worlds are no different from ours. Our students are going to question everything, and I like to think that we and they will be better for it.

Appendix

Example Text Sets

Citation information for the Next Generation Science Standards (NGSS Lead States, 2013) and the College, Career, and Civic Life (C3) Framework for Social Studies State Standards (NCSS, 2017) can be found in the References section. Each text set includes guiding questions, content standards, and an alphabetical list of resources with brief descriptions.

TEXT SET #1: ADAPTING TO SURVIVE (GRADE 3)

Guiding question: How do living things adapt to survive in their environment?
Standards (NGSS Lead States, 2013):

- Grade 3, LS4.B: Sometimes the differences in characteristics between individuals of the same species provide advantages in surviving, finding mates, and reproducing.
- Grade 3, LS4.C: For any particular environment, some kinds of organisms survive well, some survive less well, and some cannot survive at all.

Resources:
Beck, W. H. (2016). *Glow: Animals with their own nightlights.* Boston, MA: Houghton Mifflin Harcourt.
- Accompanied by vivid photographs, this book shows how bioluminescence helps animals catch prey and dodge predators.
Jenkins, S., and Page, R. (2014). *Creature features: 25 animals explain why they look the way they do*. Boston, MA: Houghton Mifflin Harcourt.
- This picture book briefly explains how various features, such as tusks and spots, help animals survive.

Jenkins, S., and Page, R. (2016). *Flying frogs and walking fish*. Boston, MA: Houghton Mifflin Harcourt.
  • The ways animals move to escape danger and protect themselves are related in this picture book.
Johnson, R. L. (2015). *When lunch fights back: Wickedly clever animal defenses*. Minneapolis, MN: Millbrook Press.
  • Short chapters show a variety of defenses animals use to evade predators, from bursting toxic bubbles to producing slime.
Mission adaptation. (2010). Retrieved from http://www.planet-science.com/catego ries/under-11s/games/2010/09/mission-adaptation.aspx.
  • In this game, students take photographs of animals and choose which adaptation allows the animal to survive in its environment. Brief explanations describe how the adaptation encourages the animal's survival.
Sydenham, S., and Thomas, R. (2015). *Adaptations*. Retrieved from http://www .kidcyber.com.au/adaptation/.
  • This website provides a clear explanation of how adaptations allow animals to survive and gives examples of animal and plant adaptations.
White Lake School (Producer). (2009, January 9). *Amazing animal adaptations* [Audio podcast]. Retrieved from https://whitelake.k12.sd.us/elementaryComput ers/Podcasts/5thGradeAnimalAdaptations.mp3.
  • This brief podcast for children and by children describes ways that animals adapt to their environments.

TEXT SET #2: CREATING AND DEPLOYING THE ATOMIC BOMB (GRADES 6–8)

Guiding questions: What were the short-term and long-term consequences of President Truman's decision to drop the atomic bomb on Hiroshima and Nagasaki? Was Truman's decision justifiable to people in 1945? Is his decision justifiable to people in contemporary times?
Standards (NCSS, 2017):

  • D2.His.4.6-8: Analyze multiple factors that influenced the perspectives of people during different historical times.
  • D2.His.14.6-8: Explain multiple causes and effects of events and developments in the past.

Resources:
Gingold, C. (1994, January). "Rain of ruin." *Cobblestone*, 15, 37–40.
  • This article describes the impact of the atomic bomb on the citizens of Hiroshima.
"Ike on Ike" [review of the book *Mandates for change: 1953–1956*, by D. Eisenhower]. (1963, November 11). *Newsweek*, 107–110.
  • A section of this book review quotes from President Eisenhower's diary, offering his candid opinion of Truman's decision to drop the atomic bomb.

Sheinkin, S. (2012). *Bomb: The race to build—and steal—the world's most danger-ous weapon*. New York: Roaring Brook Press.
- This chapter book relates the building of the atomic bomb as well as the im-pact it had on Japanese citizens and the "Father of the Atomic Bomb" himself, J. Robert Oppenheimer.

Stelson, C. (2016). *Sachiko: A Nagasaki bomb survivor's story*. Minneapolis: Carol-rhoda.
- This biography relates the impact of the Nagasaki bomb on six-year-old Sachiko and her family, revealing the human cost of war in the atomic age.

Stimson, H. L. (1947). *The decision to use the atomic bomb*. Retrieved from http://afe.easia.columbia.edu/ps/japan/stimson_harpers.pdf.
- Originally published in *Harper's Magazine*, this article outlines the reasons why the United States deployed the atomic bomb.

US War Department. (1946). *A tale of two cities* [video file]. Retrieved from http://www.learnnc.org/lp/editions/nchist-worldwar/5963 or https://archive.org/details/TaleofTw1946.
- This video describes the destruction the atomic bomb wreaked on Hiroshima and Nagasaki.

TEXT SET #3: YOUTH INVOLVEMENT IN CIVIL RIGHTS (GRADES 9–12)

Guiding questions: In what ways were young people involved in the Civil Rights Movement of the 1950s and 1960s? In what ways were their actions effective (or not)?

Standard (NCSS, 2017):

- D2.Civ.6.9-12: Evaluate citizens' and institutions' effectiveness in ad-dressing political and social problems at the local, state, tribal, national, and/or international level.

Resources:

Bausum, A. (2006). *Freedom riders: John Lewis and Jim Zwerg on the front lines of the Civil Rights Movement*. Washington, DC: National Geographic.
- This book explains the roles of John Lewis, Jim Zwerg, and other Nashville stu-dents in the 1961 Freedom Rides to desegregate public transportation.

Galan, H. (Producer/Director). (1996). *Chicano!: History of the Mexican Ameri-can Civil Rights Movement* [Motion picture]. United States: Galan Incorporated Television and Film. Retrieved from https://www.kanopystreaming.com/product/chicano-history-mexican-american-civil-rig.
- Episode 3, "Taking Back the Schools," documents the student-led protests for equity in eastern Los Angeles high schools.

Hoose, P. (2009). *Claudette Colvin: Twice toward justice*. New York: Square Fish.
- This well-researched biography explains the role of teenage Claudette Colvin in ending segregation on Montgomery city buses.

Ketcheshawno, M. (Executive Producer), Plutte, J. (Producer), and Fortier, J. M. (Director). (2001). *Alcatraz is not an island* [Motion picture]. United States: Diamond Island Productions.
- This documentary depicts activists' occupation of Alcatraz in 1969 to draw attention to Native American rights and sovereignty.

Levinson, C. (2012). *We've got a job: The 1963 Birmingham Children's March.* Atlanta, GA: Peachtree.
- Told from the perspectives of four young people who participated, this narrative offers a detailed look at the Children's March of May 1963 and the results of their actions.

Lowery, L. B., Leacock, E., Buckley, S., and Loughran, P. J. (2016). *Turning 15 on the road to freedom: My story of the 1965 Selma Voting Rights March.* New York: SPEAK.
- In clear, direct prose, Lynda Blackmon Lowery reflects on her involvement with the civil rights movement.

Wilson, T. V., and Frey, H. (Producers). (2013, September 16). *Mendez v. Westminster* [Audio podcast]. Retrieved from http://www.missedinhistory.com/podcasts/mendez-v-westminster.htm#.
- This fifty-two-minute podcast relates the story of the Mendez family and their children, who fought against school segregation in a California district during the 1940s.

TEXT SET #4: US PRESIDENTS (GRADES 3–4)

Guiding questions: What power does the president of the United States have and how was the office established? Who are the presidents of the United States?

Standards (NCSS, 2017):

- D2.Civ.1.3-5: Distinguish the responsibilities and powers of government officials at various levels and branches of government and in different times and places.
- D2.Civ.5.3-5: Explain the origins, functions, and structure of different systems of government, including those created by the United States and state institutions.

Resources:

Babwin, D. (2014, October 8). *Historian retells tale of rare Lincoln photo.* Retrieved from https://www.tweentribune.com/article/junior/historian-retells-tale-rare-lincoln-photo/.
- Available at multiple reading levels, this article shares the background behind a photograph of Abraham Lincoln in his coffin discovered by a teenager nearly one hundred years after Lincoln's death.

Bodette, M. (Producer). (2016, October 14). *Who invented the president?* [Audio podcast]. Retrieved from http://digital.vpr.net/post/who-invented-president#stream/0. Accessed: March 28, 2018.

• This podcast episode answers children's questions, including who invented the president, which country had the first president, and that first president's name.

BrainPOP. (n.d.). *U.S. presidents*. Retrieved from https://www.brainpop.com/social studies/uspresidents/.

• Videos about many US presidents and the presidential office are available on this website. Additionally, there are lesson plans, games, quizzes, and other activities associated with the topics in the videos.

Edwards, R. (2009). *Who was George Washington?* New York: Grossett & Dunlap.

• This chapter book is a biography of George Washington's life written on a level accessible to upper elementary students. Illustrations and diagrams accompanying the text are included.

Library of Congress. (n.d.). *U.S. presidents*. Retrieved from http://www.americas library.gov/aa/presidents.php.

• This website provides short biographies and timelines of some past presidents of the United States.

St. George, J., and Small, D. (2004). *So you want to be president?* New York: Philomel Books.

• Paired with entertaining illustrations, interesting and quirky facts about various presidents of the United States are revealed in this picture book.

TEXT SET #5: IMPACT OF
HURRICANE KATRINA (GRADES 3–4)

Guiding questions: How did Hurricane Katrina impact people, animals, and the environment? What could have been done to lessen the impact of the hurricane?

Standards (NGSS Lead States, 2013):

• Grade 3, ESS3.B: A variety of natural hazards result from natural processes. Humans cannot eliminate natural hazards but can take steps to reduce their impacts.
• Grade 4, ESS3.B: A variety of hazards result from natural processes (e.g., earthquakes, tsunamis, volcanic eruptions). Humans cannot eliminate the hazards but can take steps to reduce their impacts.

Beasley, L. (Producer/Director), Johnson, B. (Producer), and Colton, R.C. (Executive Producer). (2008). *Katrina's children* [Motion picture]. United States: Shadow Pictures. Retrieved from http://www.snagfilms.com/films/title/katrinas_children.

- In this documentary for kids, children explain what it was like to experience Hurricane Katrina and how it affected them.

Coleman, J. W., and Nascimbene, Y. (2013). *Eight dolphins of Katrina: A true tale of survival.* Boston, MA: Houghton Mifflin Books for Children.

- This picture book explains the rescue of eight dolphins who were lost when Hurricane Katrina slammed into the Mississippi coast.

Larson, K., Nethery, M., and Cassels, J. (2008). *Two Bobbies: A true story of Hurricane Katrina, friendship, and survival.* New York: Walker & Company.

- A story of a cat and dog surviving Hurricane Katrina's aftermath is related in this picture book.

Miller, M. (2006). *Hurricane Katrina strikes the Gulf Coast: Disaster and survival.* Berkeley Heights, NJ: Enslow Publishers.

- This short chapter book addresses how hurricanes form and the devastation Hurricane Katrina caused for people on the Gulf Coast.

National Geographic. (2010). *Hurricane Katrina pictures: Then & now, ruin & rebirth.* Retrieved from http://news.nationalgeographic.com/news/2010/08/photogalleries/100826-hurricane-katrina-pictures-fifth-anniversary-nation-before-after/.

- This photo gallery of before-and-after images allows children to visualize the destruction created by Hurricane Katrina.

WLOX [WLOX-TV]. (2015, May 21). *WLOX Katrina: Before, after, and now* [Video file]. Retrieved from https://www.youtube.com/watch?v=Tv4S2Eshy-g.

- Produced by a news station in southern Mississippi, this moving video highlights the damage Hurricane Katrina caused to coastal communities.

About the Editors

Vivian Yenika-Agbaw is professor of children's literature in the Department of Curriculum and Instruction at the Pennsylvania State University, University Park, where she teaches undergraduate and graduate courses in children's/adolescent literature. She has published numerous articles and authored/co-edited several books, including *Adolescents Rewrite Their Worlds: Using Literature to Illustrate Writing Forms* (Rowman & Littlefield, 2015); *African Youth in Contemporary Literature and Popular Culture: Identity Quest; Fairy Tales with a Black Consciousness: Essays on Adaptations of Familiar Stories*. She has taught children's literature in the Departments of Curriculum and Instruction and English at state universities in Pennsylvania (Clarion and Bloomsburg), and has taught high school English abroad and in the United States. Yenika-Agbaw has served on several editorial boards and reviewed manuscripts for *Children's Literature in Education*, *Children's Literature*, and the *Journal of Children's Literature*. She is currently serving on the International Research Society for Children's Literature Board (2017–2019). Yenika-Agbaw is also an active member of the National Council of Teachers of English (NCTE) and of the Children's Literature Association (ChLA).

Ruth McKoy Lowery is professor of literacy and associate chair of the Department of Teaching and Learning at the Ohio State University. She teaches courses on children's literature and literacy education. Her current research focuses on children's literature, particularly immigrant and multicultural literature, the adaptation of immigrant and at-risk students in schools, and preparing teachers to teach a diverse student population. Dr. Lowery is an active member of the National Council of Teachers of English (NCTE), the

International Literacy Association (ILA), and the United States Board on Books for Young People (USBBY).

Laura Anne Hudock is a PhD candidate in curriculum and instruction at the Pennsylvania State University, where she instructs pre-service teachers in children's literature, reading, and language arts courses. She also teaches in Penn State's World Campus program on the art of picture books and fantasy children's literature. Laura has presented papers at national and international conferences on picture books and reader responses to them. In 2016, she co-authored a chapter with Dr. Dan Hade, "Redefining the Early Reader in an Era of Multiliteracies: Visual Language of Mo Willems' Elephant and Piggie Series," in *The Early Reader in Children's Literature and Culture: Theorizing Books for Beginning Readers*, edited by Miskec and Wannamaker. Previously, Laura taught first grade for a decade in Virginia at a Title I elementary school and in Florida.

Paul H. Ricks is a doctoral candidate in curriculum and instruction at the Pennsylvania State University, where he currently teaches children's literature courses. Last year, he was a visiting instructor of children's literature at Brigham Young University, and prior to that he also taught fifth and sixth grade in Salt Lake City, Utah, for seven years. Through international teaching experiences in Mozambique and Brazil, Paul developed interests in cross-cultural studies and translations of Spanish and Portuguese texts. His articles have appeared in *The Dragon Lode*, *Literacy Research and Instruction*, *The Reading Teacher*, and *Literacy Today*.

About the Contributors

Kaybeth Calabria has worked in the field of special education for forty years. Her varied career includes working as an early intervention teacher, serving adults with disabilities in sheltered workshops and group homes, providing services as a school psychologist, and developing and teaching a community-based classroom for high school students with disabilities. In 1998, the Ohio Department of Education presented Kaybeth with the Franklin B. Walter Outstanding Educator Award. For the past eleven years she has had the privilege of teaching and working at Franciscan University of Steubenville. She is currently the director for the Advancement of Teaching Excellence. The role of a college professor has allowed her to engage in researching, writing, and presenting on topics of special education, teacher education, and literacy. Her favorite literacy project has been to work with pre-service teachers in coordinating inclusive literacy circles with middle school youth.

Lesley Colabucci is an associate professor of early, middle, and exceptional education at Millersville University of Pennsylvania. She teaches graduate and undergraduate classes in children's literature with a focus on diverse literature and response to literature. She has served on the American Library Association's Coretta Scott King and Geisel Award juries. She is currently a member of the National Council of Teachers of English (NCTE) Excellence in Poetry committee. She is a regular contributor to the International Literacy Association's (IRA) *Literacy Daily* book review blog. Her recent presentations and publications have included topics such as the portrayal of adoption in children's books, clustering books to meet NCSS standards, and using technology to enhance reader response.

Patricia A. Crawford is an associate professor at the University of Pittsburgh, with appointments in the early childhood education and language, literacy, and culture programs. She also serves as the associate chair for the Department of Instruction and Learning. Her current scholarly interests center on the ways in which authentic literature represents and problematizes social issues in the lives of children. Her writing has appeared in a variety of journals including *Journal of Research in Childhood Education, Early Childhood Education Journal, Young Children,* and *Childhood Education.* She is past chair of the Publications Committee for the Association for Childhood Education International and serves on the editorial boards of *Journal of Research in Childhood Education, Dragon Lode, Early Childhood Education Journal, The Reading Teacher,* and *Literacy Research and Instruction.*

Margot Dickey is an elementary specialist in the Advanced Academic Programs (gifted education) for Fairfax County Public Schools. She has thirteen years of experience as an elementary educator, teaching second- and third-grade general education students, third-grade self-contained gifted students, and gifted resource K–5. Having taught exclusively in Title I schools, Margot is passionate about identifying student strengths and providing nurturance and access to advanced materials to historically underrepresented students. Margot graduated from James Madison University with a degree in early childhood education. She also has an endorsement in gifted education.

Danling Fu, PhD, is professor of language and culture in the School of Teaching and Learning, College of Education at the University of Florida. She researches and provides in-service and consultancy to public schools nationally, with a special focus on literacy instruction for English language learners/emergent bilinguals. For a decade, she worked in New York City schools with a high percentage of new immigrant students and low graduation rates. She serves on the National Advisory Board for the CUNY-New York State Initiative on emergent bilinguals. Her publications include six books and more than one hundred journal articles, book chapters, and book reviews addressing literacy instruction for new immigrant students and literacy instruction in cross-cultural contexts.

Danielle Hartsfield is assistant professor in the Elementary/Special Education program at the University of North Georgia. She graduated from Old Dominion University in 2014 with a PhD in curriculum and instruction. Prior to her doctoral studies, she was a fourth-grade teacher. Her research interests include children's literature as well as teachers' beliefs about censorship and intellectual freedom. Danielle is active in the Association for Library Service to Children and the Children's Literature and Reading Special Interest Group of the International Literacy Association.

Nicole Maxwell is an assistant professor in the Elementary/Special Education (ELE/SPED) program at the University of North Georgia. She also serves as co-coordinator of the ELE/SPED program. Her research interests include reading and literacy instruction, integrating literacy in the content areas, and the influence of participation in a literacy lab on undergraduate teacher candidates. Previously, Nicole worked in elementary education for ten years as a first-grade and Early Intervention program teacher, in kindergarten through fifth grade. She is a member of the Georgia Association of Teacher Educators (GATE) Executive Committee. Nicole has presented locally and nationally.

Cuthbert Rowland-Storm is a father, an elementary school educator in West Seattle, and a doctoral candidate in Language, Culture, and Society and the English Language Arts Education departments of the Pennsylvania State University's College of Education. His work focuses on how difference is made to matter in schools, books, and other texts.

Deborah L. Thompson, PhD, is professor emeritus at the College of New Jersey in Ewing, New Jersey. During her college tenure, Dr. Thompson taught courses in emergent and early literacy, elementary and middle school reading instruction, secondary content reading, adolescent and children's literature—multicultural and traditional. She conducted numerous professional development workshops on effective reading and writing instruction, using children's literature (traditional and multicultural) in the classroom, and using nonfiction in the classroom. Her writing and research areas included exploring cross-cultural connections in folklore, children's responses to literature, children's early vocabulary development, and the uses of multicultural children's literature in the literacy curriculum. From 2014 to 2017, she served as co-editor of *The Dragon Lode,* the peer-reviewed journal of the Children's Literature and Reading Special Interest Group of the International Literacy Association.

Xiaodi Zhou is currently an assistant professor of reading at Georgia Southwestern State. He earned his PhD from the University of Georgia and researched the writing experiences of an early adolescent Mexican American girl from an undocumented family for his dissertation research. During and following his doctoral studies, he researched and wrote on the experiences of minority students from different cultures and how their psyches are affected by both larger globalization trends and increasing local counter-trends.

Born in China, he moved to the United States at age seven to join his mother. Throughout his life, he has visited many different countries and cultures, including South Africa, Thailand, and Europe, returning several times to China. He speaks three languages—English, Chinese, and Spanish—and enjoys learning about and immersing in different cultures and world perspectives. With his scholarship, he hopes to connect and bridge different ways of understanding and naming the world.

www.ingramcontent.com/pod-product-compliance
Lightning Source LLC
Chambersburg PA
CBHW020702030726
47498CB00002B/597